FAMILY PLANNING ON A CROWDED PLANET

FAMILY PLANNING ON A CROWDED PLANET

BY WILSON YATES

GREENWOOD PRESS, PUBLISHERS
WESTPORT, CONNECTICUT

Library of Congress Cataloging in Publication Data

Yates, Wilson.
 Family planning on a crowded planet.

 Reprint. Originally published: Minneapolis : Augsburg,
1971.
 Bibliography: p.
 Includes index.
 1. Population. 2. Family size. 3. Birth control.
4. Population--Moral and ethical aspects. I. Title.
HB871.Y34 1983   304.6'66   82-24160
ISBN 0-313-22680-6 (lib. bdg.)

Reprinted with the permission of Augsburg Publishing House

Reprinted in 1983 by Greenwood Press
A division of Congressional Information Service, Inc.
88 Post Road West, Westport, Connecticut 06881

Printed in the United States of America

10 9 8 7 6 5 4 3 2 1

To my wife, Gayle
and to my children,
Natasha and Stiles

CONTENTS

PREFACE

The story is as old as the dawn of human history. Man and woman become husband and wife and they have children. In the process they have to deal in some fashion with the question of how many children to have.

For the medieval peasant the answer may have been, "As many as God ordains."

For the American frontiersman of the 19th century, "As many as we need to fell the trees and warm the hearth with laughter."

For the Renaissance courtesan having an affair the response was unflinchingly "none."

For the young American couple the answer may be, "We are not sure given the world we live in."

This book is about the population explosion—the context in which the question of family size must be understood. The explosion is real. It is of crisis proportion. In 1800 the world population stood at less than one billion people. By the end of 1970, it had passed the 3½ billion mark. By 2010, at the present two per cent growth rate, it is estimated that it will have doubled to seven billion. For all who share this single planetary home, therefore, to speak of population is to speak of crisis.

In the first part of this study we will develop a framework for the analysis of the issue. Our specific concern, however, is to confront three major imperatives. First, we must *recognize* the population explosion as a crisis. Second, we need to *identify ourselves* and our society as part of that crisis. Third, we must be willing to *critically examine and change* certain fundamental value orientations that inform our cultural vision of the problem and the social policies we have developed in response.

This discussion is not about a problem, therefore, that lies somewhere "over there." It is about an issue to which we are inextricably bound as individuals and as a nation. We are a part of the crisis.

It is not always easy to engage people in discussion about issues of crisis proportion. Some find it impossible to differentiate crisis issues from the commonplace. Questions of life and death significance take on little more importance than ordering the day's calendar. Chatter at parties can move from tales of ecological doom to the relative merits of foreign cars to the incidents of Indochina massacres with little change in expression or tone. Television programs that portray hunger in Calcutta are interrupted by clever sales pitches for high protein dog food.

At other times we may differentiate the serious from the trivial, but our feelings and intellect have been so bombarded that we find it easier to avoid identifying with it; to accept and justify a sense of helplessness in place of aggressive participation in solving it; or, to hover within a blanket of rationalizations in which our own position becomes entrenched and closed to the issue rather than open to reevaluation and change.

Or perhaps we do identify, accept, and respond to an issue as crucial to our destiny and the destiny of our neighbor. But in the process we may bracket our consideration. We turn our recognition of it into a fad, and like a fad free ourselves from it when it no longer entices us or commands our attention.

The population crisis is no exception. It does receive attention, but often it is the detached attention people accord to issues unrelated to themselves. Television news programs deliver reports on the seriousness of the question but often follow with human interest stories such as how a woman courageously had a child though her heart condition indicated a slim chance for survival. The population problem is often considered seriously only in discussions of the "irresponsible poor" or of economic aid to overpopulated nations.

The difficulty for an individual or nation to recognize and respond to a crisis is not unique to North Americans. All ages and civilizations share in the problem, but that is no justification for inaction. It simply places before us the need for a more realistic appraisal of the issues, what we can do to respond in constructive fashion, and what factors prevent us from such response.

The imperatives we examine in this book are, at their roots, moral judgments, for they define individual and social responsibility for issues that affect the fulfillment and destiny of human life. This book invites the reader to join in serious moral discourse about our personal relationship to one of the world's major issues.

I wish to acknowledge my appreciation to my teachers, James Luther Adams and Ralph Potter, who introduced me to the significance of the population issue and guided me through a doctoral thesis on the subject; and to my wife, Gayle, whose intellectual stimulation, personal support, and touches of humor have been crucial in this undertaking.

A FRAMEWORK FOR APPROACHING THE PROBLEM

1

A newscaster interviews two persons: a sociologist who predicts that government will eventually license couples before they are allowed to have children, and a woman who says she would never obey laws that violate a right as sacred as procreation.

A book title reads *The Population Bomb*. It is followed in bold type with the statement: "While you are reading these words, four people will have died from starvation. Most of them children." [1]

A Lutheran Church in America policy statement maintains:

> People have a right not to have children without being accused of selfishness or a betrayal of the divine plan; and every child has a right to be a wanted child.
> All persons are entitled to receive from governmental and voluntary agencies information about conception control. [2]

An *Esquire* magazine article carries the title, "The Human Race Has, Maybe, Thirty-Five Years Left," [3] and a *New Republic* lead article written by a major population scientist dismisses the population explosion in America as a "nonsense explosion." [4]

Out of such fragments of conflicting opinion we make judgments about our own family size, about a realistic policy for our society and our participation with other nations in the world problem. It becomes crucially important, therefore, that we have an adequate framework for appropriating and assessing such information. Unfortunately, our framework is all too often limited and our analysis ends in cardboard cliches easily bent by sophisticated games in demographic statistics and defensive outbursts from mothers of six.

In this chapter we will develop a framework to aid us in analysis and decision-making regarding procreation and the population explosion. It will be of specific importance in helping us answer two questions: "what should I take into consideration in reasoning about the population question?" and "how do I critique the analyses of others who are debating the issue?" In laying out the framework, we will consider five major areas of concern, each of which can be introduced in the form of a question.

1. What is the relationship of the past, present, and future to the analysis of the issue?

2. What are the sources of information crucial in the analysis?

3. What type of information is relevant to the analysis?

4. What significance do theological and ideological value factors play in such an analysis?

5. What are the boundaries of moral responsibility in considering the issue?

Above all in our consideration we should remember that we are dealing with an issue that binds the very personal question of "how many children ought we to have as a couple?" to the question of "what is an appropriate world population growth rate?" There is no simple division of the issue into the classical dichotomy of personal and social. The two are one. The population of nations, continents, and the world cannot be considered without recognizing the desires and actions of couples. In turn, the decisions of couples must be related to the meaning of population growth in general or we will continue to suffer the fate of an unresolved crisis whose boundaries may be reaching the point of global disaster.

PAST, PRESENT, AND FUTURE

When we remember that the discovery of smallpox vaccine greatly altered the birth rate/death rate balance in favor of births over deaths, we realize that events in the history of population have been crucial in the creation of our present dilemma.[5] Values which emerged in past eras, such as the value of procreation as the primary purpose of marriage, are still operative and contribute to a high fertility norm in our own time. When we recognize this, we realize that the present crisis has been created and is in part maintained by historical forces.

When we learn that tonight over 600,000 people will sleep on the streets of Calcutta because there are no buildings to house them, and when we are reminded that economic advantages for Egypt resulting from the Aswan Dam have been offset by the population growth rate, we are made aware that the population issue is a present crisis.

When we are told that because of overpopulation and underproduction major nations of the Third World will experience famine unparalleled in history within a decade or less, we are faced with the reality of the future posing stark questions of life and death significance.

The population issue has three dimensions. It has a past that has helped create the crisis and continues to affect it, a present in which we confront the crisis, and a future that holds the stakes for which we must now play our hand. The importance we attach to each of these dimensions contributes to our understanding and response to the issue.

15

THE PAST. In dealing with the issue of population size, people have throughout their history developed values, perspectives, and goals that inform their present responses to the question. If you came from a family of ten and enjoyed a great deal of warmth, love, and creativity, the image of the large family as "good" might be shaping your attitude towards your own family size.

Population events in the history of societies have greatly altered the destiny of future generations. The 14th century saw the Black Death sweep across Europe destroying one-fourth of its population. This event was to affect the attitude of a continent toward population growth for centuries to come and contribute to a psychology of population scarcity. Since the 18th and 19th centuries, Americans have assumed that the United States has boundless space, unlimited opportunities, and can, therefore, absorb an endless increase in population. Today that assumption continues to influence American thought even though the "boundless," "unlimited," and "endless" conditions have long since changed.

The population history of a nation must be considered, just as the background of an individual must be studied, to understand its fertility norms and patterns of behavior. Insofar as the past has influenced their perspective and contributes to their present understanding of procreation, it has helped determine family size and national population growth rates. Therefore, it must be dealt with as one key in changing those birth rates.

THE PRESENT refers to given conditions in the world, perspectives on those conditions, and our possible responses to them. The present birth rate, the effects of population density, and the relationship between the number of people and resources are its subjects. It is the *now* where the past and the future meet. It is the arena where we come to terms with what procreation means for our own destiny.

THE FUTURE is unknown. It is the realm of possibility, in which we attempt to discern what might happen if present policies and population trends are continued. It is the subject of endless calculation and the nightmare of the Population Explosionists. It is the tomorrow that we seek to prepare for by analysis and prediction that we might survive.

In our analysis we should take all three dimensions into consideration. Thus a couple in determining the number of children they will have should recognize that they bring to the decision attitudes, values, and experiences from their past which contribute to their present decision; that the present situation has certain psychological, social, economic, and moral factors to be acknowledged; and that they are responsible for weighing their decision in terms of future possibilities for the child, themselves, and the world.

The same is true for nations as a whole. Influences of the past, present conditions, and future possibilities must be considered. If one of the dimensions is left out, the picture is distorted. The following illustrations show what happens when one dimension is emphasized and the others ignored.

In Latin America, a couple might decide to have eight or ten children because they anticipate a high infant mortality rate. In earlier years, several of the children would have died. But now improved medical treatment has caused the death rate to decline, making it likely that most of the children will survive to become adults. By understanding their situation only in terms of what has been the case in the past, however, the couple contributes to a problem that threatens their future.

Or we may take the woman who insists that she is going to have six children because her mother had six children and "no one was ever happier." This woman has "copped out" on the present and the future.

Henry C. Wallich, a *Newsweek* columnist, exhibits another form of dependence on the past when he writes:

> *Quite without outside interference, time and human nature will probably take care of the population problem. It has taken us barely a century to come down from the twelve-child family to the three-child family. Somewhere in the astronomical future, even this rate of growth would leave standing room only, and so it will not continue indefinitely.*[6]

17

This type of thinking is common in America. Because everything has supposedly gone well in the past, everything will go well in the future. This makes the past an escape from frightening problems in the present and the future. All of these examples reveal "bondage" to the past, because they fail to see the present and future as dynamic dimensions of the situation.

In turn, the person or nation who is in bondage to the present responds only to the immediate situation and its short range possibilities and goals. The future implications of the population explosion are ignored as are the historical factors that still contribute to it.

On another side are people who focus exclusively on the future, failing to appreciate the dynamics of the past or the present. Thus the health official who fully grasps the dangerous implications a high fertility rate poses for the future may, at the same time, fail to devise an effective birth control program because he has ignored the historical reasons still informing couples to bear large families.

When we ignore the future, looking only to the past, an invitation is extended to disaster. But where the past is ignored, plans posed for the future may be ineffectual.

In thinking about the population problem, therefore, we should recognize the significance of all three dimensions and avoid the tendency to orient ourselves to one, to the exclusion of the others.

SOURCES OF INFORMATION

What are the sources of information we use in assessing the population issue? Are our sources articles in popular magazines like *Newsweek* and *McCalls* or journals of opinions like the *New Republic* or the *Christian Century*? Do we turn to books like Paul Ehrlich's *The Population Bomb* or to more technical studies like David Heer's *Society and Population*? Do we look primarily to doctors, journalists, clergymen, politicians, our neighbors, or to our own experience?

There are many sources. To make rational decisions about the population question, however, we must be able to discriminate among them, and the type of information they offer. In this discussion we have two basic tasks. One is to identify the sources, acknowledging certain of their strengths and weaknesses; and the second is to suggest common factors which are critical to their analysis and to ours. In the process we shall focus on professional analysts, reformers, popular commentators, political leaders, policy implementors, and citizens.

The professional analysts—These are people whose work is oriented to the technical study of some dimension of the population question. They are located primarily in three fields: social sciences, life sciences, and humanistic studies. The *social scientists* are concerned with many dimensions of the problem, including such broad concerns as the relationship of population to human relations, institutional structures, and cultural value systems. One major figure in the field is the demographer. A definition of his field in terms of the questions he deals with will give insight into what he does.

> What is happening to the size of the population in the world as a whole, in world regions, in nations, in provinces, and in localities? What combinations of causes are responsible for population growth or decline in these units? Why do some populations grow rapidly and others more slowly? Why does one society grow at one time, and decline at another? Does our knowledge of the causes of growth provide us with means to predict the future? How do changes in the composition of a population—especially age, sex, and marital composition—affect its total rate of change? And conversely, how does total growth affect a population's composition? How are changes in a population's growth and composition related to its special distribution?[7]

Though demography has emerged as an independent field of study, many demographers work out of two other disciplines long involved with the population question: sociology and economics. The sociologist studies some of the same questions but usually focuses on the relationship of population growth and decline to cultural values and social structure. For example, a sociologist may study your value orientation toward procreation to see how it compares with those of people in other classes or societies. Or he might attempt to determine the relationship of your attitude toward family size to your attitude toward woman's role in society.

The economist looks more directly at the relationship of population change and the economic factor. He may focus on the effect of population growth on economic growth in developing countries. Or he may try to determine whether your income and the cost of rearing children actually affects the size of your family.

Other social scientists including anthropologists, psychologists, and political scientists examine procreation from their own perspectives.

The *life sciences* focus on the relationship of population to ecology, biology, oceanography, medical science, and agriculture. In the past five years, the ecologists have received a great deal of attention, especially in their evaluations of the effect of population growth on the balance of nature. Oceanographers have entered the debate in their evaluation of whether the ocean can be made a major new source of food and fuel. Medical scientists among many tasks seek more effective means of conception control.

The *humanistic sciences*. History and ethics are of critical importance. From our standpoint the ethicist's role needs particular comment. This is a role we all play insofar as we probe the moral dimension of human action as it is related to procreation and its control. The ethicist should be responsible for understanding and assessing data from the social and life sciences and ordering and critiqueing that data in terms of sources, scope, and presuppositions used in its interpretation. He must be aware of cultural values and norms related to the issue and how they affect procreation and family size. He must develop a method for making this type of assessment and analysis. In light of these tasks, he offers a critique of policy recommendations regarding population, lifting up and judging their moral implications in light of whatever criteria of moral principles he has isolated as relevant to the subject. This chapter provides an outline of a possible method.

The Reformers. Nowhere has the issue of birth control been more colorful than in the events surrounding the reformers. Books have been banned, laws passed, demonstrations held, and people jailed for its cause. In this process, the reformer has played two crucial roles: critic and advocate. Historically he has been concerned with the battles over legitimizing birth control as not only morally justifiable but morally obligatory. The categories *responsible* and *planned* parenthood imply that family size is a question of rational control and a demand for its practice. Reform movements began to make an impact in this century particularly under the leadership of Margaret Sanger and were institutionalized eventually into such bodies as Planned Parenthood/World Population and the Population Council, with broad based programs aimed at achieving a controlled population growth rate.

The reformer's style is different from that of the professional analyst. He may rely on the analyst for interpretation and judgment regarding technical data and social policy but he frames his own case to accommodate his own goals. He wishes to see change occur and his methods may include conversion, pressure, or propagandizing. He might be a prophet or a lobbyist. He might be the instigator of new explorations and actions in the population field insofar as he pressures both professional analyst and politician to probe the issue in greater depth. Or he may be at the other end of the track, pressuring an effective implementation of policies that already have been agreed upon.

The Popular Commentator is usually a journalist or layman who has chosen to write or speak on the subject. He deals with the question because of its significance at the moment. He may rely heavily on perspectives developed by others, such as professional analysts and reformers. He might disseminate information about the subject as a newsworthy item or make comment on the issue, taking a stand in the process. Because journalism involves the dissemination of information in condensed form to a mass audience, its style invites broad generalization and limited documentation.

The style, therefore, is limited, but also good in its ability to accent specific dimensions of a question. Above all, the press provides in its variety a sounding board and debate tournament, giving the issue wide and popular hearing. Thus we find the issue in as unsuspected a place as a Dear Abby column which carried the heading "Don't Put on Heirs." A woman writes:

> Dear Abby: I would like to pass along a little advice to the young mother who was so upset over having to tell her mother they were expecting their third child in five years. When I told my little 96-year-old mother that my daughter was expecting her fourth child, she looked at me and smiled, and said, "It is always nicer to put an extra chair up to the table than to take one away."
>
> Macon, Mo.

And Abby replies:

> Dear Missouri: Your 96-year-old mother was probably thinking about the days of her youth when another child meant another much needed farmhand. Today, if somebody doesn't blow the whistle on the birth rate, we won't need any chairs.[8]

Popular commentators are important because most people tend to form their opinions on the basis of evidence given in mass media presentations. The danger is that too little information will be gained from other sources to balance the limited presentation of the media.

Political Leaders. Political leaders deal with population control as a policy question for legislative action. Should contraceptives be free to everyone? Should foreign aid be tied to birth control policies? Should the state tax families bearing more than two children? Should policies be designed to encourage couples to adopt after they have had two children?

Some political leaders, such as Congressman Udall of Arizona, have become well-informed decision makers. Most often, however, the leaders are highly dependent on professional analysts and various interest groups for information. From our standpoint, it suggests that we should be aware of who influences government officials and elected representatives and in what particular directions. We should be concerned about their sources of information and patterns of decision making.

The Implementors. The social worker in a Minneapolis Neighborhood House who provides free family planning information, and the public health nurse establishing a birth control clinic in India are implementors of policy. Implementors include public health officials, social workers, church agency leaders, government agency bureaucrats, or nurses and doctors who transform policy into operating programs.

The Citizens. We all are the citizens who must inform ourselves of the issue and its implications for ourselves and for our world. The development and maintenance of an adequate population policy is dependent on us.

Thus with our attitudes, judgments, and practices we are the subjects of the professional analyst's research. We are the targets of the reformer's arguments, the media people's commentaries, and the politician's considerations in decision making. But we can also be participants in dealing with the crisis through the institutions we belong to by effecting population policies and practices; and, above all, we are participants as child-bearers who must decide how many children we can justifiably bring into the world.

Given these groups, we can note certain characteristics they all share.

(1) All these analysts depend on institutions to present their cases. The professional analyst is normally a part of an academic institution. Centers for population studies have emerged within university systems and courses in population can be found in institutions ranging from state colleges to theological seminaries.

The reformer has his movement or his institution, the commentator his communication medium, the politician his legislative bodies and government agencies, the implementor his organizational structures both private and public, and the citizen his voluntary associations. When, then, we examine sources we should remain aware that we are not dealing only with individuals but with institutions that channel information, debate issues, and develop and implement policy. In effect, insofar as we are respondents to a crisis, we are dependent ultimately on institutional structures which in a democratic society constitute the centers of power and action.

(2) These various types of analysts might have several functions. The medical doctor may also wear the cloak of reformer, as does Dr. Allan Gutemacher, a leader in planned parenthood. The popular commentator and reformer, Paul Ehrlich, author of *The Population Bomb* is a biologist.

(3) Ralph Potter, the Harvard social ethicist, has observed that in the decision-making process, certain loyalties and commitments must be recognized. He writes:

> *Affirmation of loyalty also affects policy thought. Consciously or unconsciously, men make decisions regarding what shall be taken as their primary object of concern. They create expressive symbols which represent a center of value, locus of commitment, or source of identity. It makes a difference whether they are dedicated to a nation, an ideology, a church, "humanity," an ideal community, or some other object of loyalty.*[9]

We should ask, therefore, where our analyst's fundamental commitment regarding the issue actually lies. Is it with a disinterested research commitment to scientific analysis? To a population council? To a church body? Is it to a political constituency which may tend for religious reasons to be either very open to the development of comprehensive population policies or to be rigidly opposed? Can we discern certain commitments, loyalties, or interests that may tend to focus the analysis in a particular direction?

(4) Finally, these sources affect social policy as well as individual attitudes through the styles, media, institutional structures, or personal behavior which they have access to or reveal in practice.

24

We can translate the above discussion into five questions for use in developing our framework:

1. *What is the source?*

2. *What institution or profession is the source associated with?*

3. *What function does the source have? Analyst? Reformer? Commentator?*

4. *What are the commitments and loyalties of the source? How do they affect the information that the source provides?*

5. *How does the source affect the developing or implementing of social policy?*

Overall, we should remain open to the spectrum of sources in our decision-making, and be critical of any analysis which is too dependent on a limited source.

KINDS OF INFORMATION RELEVANT TO THE ANALYSIS

Part of the problem with an issue as complex as the population crisis is that there may be more information than an individual can easily appropriate and respond to. Three questions help us sort out and order the material available:

(1) What population theories are at work?

(2) What are the related factors relevant to population analysis?

(3) What factors did the analyst consider?

(1) *What population theories are operative in the analysis?* Certain working theories used in population analysis should be recognized. Some are quite broad, others are narrowed to one particular dimension of the population problem. We will take three theoretical perspectives commonly used in studies on population. Each is related to understanding population growth and control and should be a part of our working knowledge in dealing with the issue.[10]

25

The first theoretical framework is the *birth rate/death rate differential* in which we approach the analysis of population by observing changes in these rates. Population growth is calculated in terms of the increase or decrease per 1000. Until 1800 a rough balance between the birth rate and the death rate kept the population steady. After 1800 the death rate began to drop. In many countries there has been a decrease in the birth rate but greater decrease in the death rate. Thus the population has grown. In Third World countries a birth rate of 40 to 45 per 1000 is high because the death rate is only 15 to 20 per 1000."[11]

A second framework is focused on *population growth in relation to resources.* Here the population crisis is defined in terms of whether there are enough resources to meet present and future demands. When the issue is broadened the ecological question becomes a dominant one: what effect will a given level of resource consumption have on the environmental balance of nature? This framework is helpful because it shows us that the population crisis is not just a matter of numbers but size in relationship to available resources and ecological balance.

A third theoretical framework often referred to is the *theory of demographic transition.* This theory maintains that population changes have gone through four stages with a different effect on population growth. One analyst summarizes the stages in these terms:

> *Stage 1: High death rates and equally high birth rates. Resultant rate of population growth: zero.*
>
> *Stage 2: Decline of death rates but not of birth rates. Resultant rate of growth: positive and increasing.*
>
> *Stage 3: Continued decline of death rates and decline of birth rates. Resultant rate of growth: positive but no longer increasing.*
>
> *Stage 4: Low death rates and equally low birth rates. Resultant rate of growth: diminishing toward zero.*[12]

In this transition it is argued that industrialization and

urbanization contribute to both the decline in the death rate and then in the birth rate. The drop in birth rate occurs more slowly, however, declining only after it becomes apparent that in an industrialized urban situation a high birth rate works an economic hardship on families.

This theory is an important one, but it has not proved as adequate as once thought. The major reason is that after World War II the United States and other countries that had supposedly completed the transition experienced rising birth rates.

The theory is still helpful, but it should not be made into a law of inevitable consequences. Changes do occur and the stages are not as stable as they would indicate even in later refined versions which have attempted to take some of the changes into consideration.

There are many other theoretical schemes regarding population, its changes, and relationships. This discussion presents only certain familiar frameworks. These theories are important because they provide categories, explain relationships, and identify trends that are helpful in interpreting and developing a perspective on the issue.

(2) *What are the related factors relevant to population analysis?* Certain factors related to procreation are important in understanding its significance. If I say I do not wish to have children because the health of my wife might be endangered, or because I am unable to assure the child a psychologically and economically stable home life, I have introduced three crucial factors in my reasoning: the physical, the psychological, and the economic.

Here we will acknowledge briefly certain major relational factors and in so doing develop a "working" spectrum of areas relevant to the population issue.

a. One factor is the *demographic.* We have already touched on the role of the demographer in population analysis and examined the central thesis of demography. A further example of demographic information is this chart and the conclusions drawn from it in the caption.[13]

27

Population Dilemma: The Poorer Nations Have the Higher Birth Rates

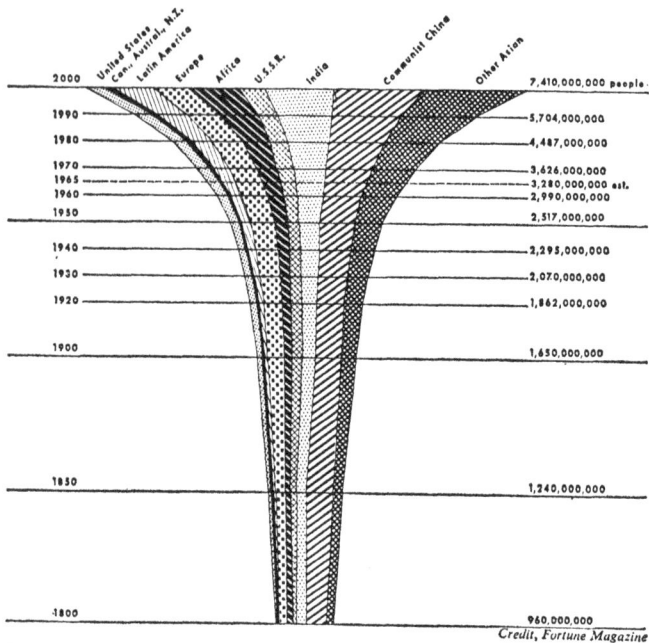

Credit, Fortune Magazine

*A new graph developed to show population growth and projections is shaped.
like a long-stemmed urn which flares broadly as it approaches the year 2000.
Most of the flare is caused by the poorer parts of the world, while only slight
expansions are projected for the U.S., Canada, Australia, New Zealand,
and Europe. That is because the poorer nations have the fastest growth rates.*

b. The economic factor is closely related to the question of population. Thomas Malthus, a late 18th century economist and clergyman, in his classical study *On Population*, introduced major issues relevant to the question. Serious study of population following Malthus was, until recently, primarily a dimension of economic analysis. A basic concern of economics has been the effect of population on economic development—this question has been important in the contemporary debate. Where is population growth essential for development? When does it cancel development gains?

Another example is the effect of economic conditions on the decision to have children. In America, the birth rate dipped during the depression of the 1930s. Sylvia

Porter, an economist and journalist, suggests that the rising cost of child care will be a major variable in limiting the present American birth rate.

> Following up on a column I wrote back in April emphasizing how much it costs to raise a child, the Institute of Life Insurance (ILI) in New York has sharply increased its estimates of the costs of raising a child merely to the age of 18. The new estimate is $30,000 —and that's for one kid, allows no frills such as private school, orthodontia, summer trip abroad. . . .
>
> Will the high cost of merely feeding a child today be a factor in the downward trend in family size? Not to mention the expenses of housing the kids, transporting them, keeping them healthy, educating them?
>
> Will this be, as I suspect, a much more powerful factor for population control than is yet recognized?[14]

The economic factor is closely related to the question of population. The economy and population size mutually affect one another.

c. *Sociological information* is crucial in relating population growth to institutions such as the family and social patterns of interaction. Sudden population growth on the edge of a city can place major strains on the town's institutions as they try to keep up with greater demands on housing, schools, streets, water, and parks. In turn, the boarded buildings, closed depot, and empty houses of many small towns show the correlation between a community's death and the decline of population.[15]

d. The *political factor* involves the relationship of political structures and social policy to population. For example, how does density of population affect political structures? What is the relationship between population size and citizen involvement in political decision-making? Political factors are also important in formulating policy related to the development of family planning.[16]

e. *The psychological dimension* is another important factor. For example, what is the psychological effect on people who live in densely populated areas? Will it make people cannibalistic, as some have predicted? Or will we learn to interact in new but humane ways?

f. An area of recent consideration is *ecology*. Population is important in understanding and dealing with the ecological question and ecologists are some of the most radical birth control advocates. Most troubling to them is the fear that human population can unbalance nature, turning it back upon man with devastating consequences. How many lakes can we kill, how much pollution can we release into the air, how much of the environment can we destroy and remake in our own image before we destroy ourselves? [17]

g. A further factor is *medical*. This is important in terms of the individual's health, and the public health of society. Procreation obviously has a direct relationship to the physical health of the mother. The question becomes more complex when we start exploring genetic questions. For example, should mentally retarded couples reproduce?

On public health questions the scope broadens. With the prediction of mass famine in the 1970s and 80s and the possible reemergence of certain diseases which feed off the starving, the whole field of public health becomes most significant.

h. *Technology* is important to population control at two levels. It is asked to provide inexpensive and effective means of birth control. Birth control will not bring the birth rate down, of course, if control itself is not desired, but the necessary decrease is equally unlikely without improved means of control.

The technology of birth control is not new. The ancient Egyptians experimented with crocodile dung, the Romans with a lemon extract. Before rubber, condoms were made of animal skin membrane. Madame de Stael provided a critical commentary on the level of technological progress in this area when she said that the sheath "provided a cobweb of protection and a bulwark against love." Progress has been made but still there is no method which meets the demand of mass population control.[18]

Technology is also related to population at a second level. A technological society requires more economic, social, and natural resources per-capita than less well-developed countries. Thus, technology contributes to overpopulation by increasing the resource consumption rate in a given population. In this way, wealthier nations with relatively low birth rates but high consumption levels contribute as much to the crisis as poorer nations with larger population but lower consumption.

j. A final factor is the *cultural factor*. This has to do with overarching theological and ideological beliefs and the values and norms which manifest them. When you say, "I have a right to have as many children as I want," a normative judgment has been made which is grounded in your moral and religious belief system. Such beliefs are crucial to our understanding of and reactions to procreation and population control.

(3) *What range of information is used by the analyst in substantiating his argument?*

There is always the danger that analysts will fail to look at as broad a range of information as they should. Thus, sweeping conclusions are made from an analysis that has been limited to one type of data. Readers of population studies should always ask, "What spheres are being left out that should be included?"

For example, the analyst who insists, as many do, that the United States has plenty of room for population expansion and therefore doesn't really have a population problem should be challenged not only for what he has said but for what he has ignored. The issue is not only geographical space but the quality of life within that space.

Or, to take another example, when an analyst says the population problem can be solved by producing more adequate contraceptives, he has assumed that people *want* to control family size. He has ignored the fact that contraceptives are helpful only when a couple *desires* to practice birth control. He has ignored the whole area of cultural value orientations and preferences.[19]

Furthermore, in an examination of population we can look at the factors given above as well as other factors in light of a range of subjects: the individual, the family, the group, the nation, the world. If, then, we were to have the full range of data and relational subjects we would examine each of the factors as it might relate to each of the subjects. A diagram of this may help illustrate:

FACTORS	SUBJECTS
Demographic	Individual
Economic	
Sociological	Family
Political	
Psychological	Group
Ecological	
Medical	Nation
Technological	
Cultural	World

CULTURAL BELIEFS AND VALUES WHICH AFFECT THE ISSUE

Cultural beliefs refer to the theological and ideological beliefs and value orientations which we hold regarding procreation and its significance for personal, social, and natural life. As theologians and sociologists of religion have often stated, there is a basic correlation between patterns of behavior and belief systems which inform and legitimate that behavior.

We can understand the role of cultural values in the analysis of population in two ways. The first relates to the basic ideological presuppositions which lie behind the methods and conclusions of analysis regarding the population issue. The second is the application of values to procreation and population growth.

The first involves an answer to the question, what basic ideological presuppositions are at work in the analyst's own examination? Some analysts, particularly from the scientific field, say that their approach is free of ideological values and suppositions. Certainly we have a right to expect that they use care in isolating and examining the information to avoid distortions. At the same time, however, scientific disciplines, and particularly the social sciences, begin with presuppositions about man, society, freedom, justice, and equality. These presuppositions lie behind what otherwise might appear to be rehearsals of "facts." They should be acknowledged by the analyst, but most of the time they are not. Consequently, we have to lift them out for closer examination before we allow them to become crucial to our own conclusions about the issue.[20]

The second role of cultural factors is more explicit in the process of analysis and decision-making. People tend to ground the meaning of procreation in their theological or ideological concepts of God, order, change, and purpose that they hold. The Christian, for example, may say that procreation is a divinely ordained process in the world for man's own perpetuation. Some Christians see procreation and its control as participating in the creative process, responsibly fulfilling the will of God. But even Christians are divided. For many Roman Catholics, procreation has been understood as the primary purpose of marriage. This has also been true for certain Protestants but for mainline American Protestants, the primary purpose of marriage is companionship—procreation is the natural blessing of the relationship.[21] This difference has contributed historically to the more flexible stance within Protestantism on the question of birth control.

Arthur Dyke, in an article on "Religious Factors in the Population Problem," explores the significance of religious belief for procreation. He demonstrates that all major religions have beliefs, symbols, and values which play into the decision making process.

> Religious beliefs or belief systems can influence the person's perceptual and behavioral responses of his environment in at least two very basic ways: they induce the believer to have certain definite expectations of his environment both in the form of circumstances that permit the perpetuation of his religion through ritual, and in the form of blessings or rewards

33

for piety; secondly, they provide the believer with an orientation to the environment both in the form of more or less explicit views of the role of man and of God in shaping events in nature and in history, and in the form of a certain personality type. Each of these religiously prompted relations to one's environment has bearing in one way or another upon the motivation governing the decisions to control family size and hence, upon actual birth rates.[22]

Theological and ideological beliefs and values inform our responses to the issue, making significant contribution in the process of decision-making.[23]

THE BOUNDARIES OF MORAL CONCERN

We dealt earlier with the need to remain open to a range of data regarding our decision-making.

Here our concern shifts to the question of how inclusive we are in defining the boundaries of moral responsibility. To what and to whom are we accountable in our moral deliberation? This cannot be answered by setting predetermined limits since moral demands change with situational and historical conditions. Nevertheless, the boundaries of moral deliberation should be as inclusive as possible.

This means that moral deliberation about the question of family size should take into consideration responsibility to the unconceived child, to the other children in the family, the marriage partner, the nation, the global community, to the environment, and to God as the source of creation. It is here, however, that we come to one of the most difficult issues in our entire consideration, for one of the marked characteristics of deliberation regarding procreation is the extent to which boundaries already have been established before the deliberations actually take place. Thus responsibility has been oriented to wife or husband or to the child or to a socio-economic or ethnic group and limited to these parties. We should be self-conscious, therefore, about how these boundaries are defined.

SUMMARY

Our goal is a working framework to analyze the population crisis and its related issues. The following diagram summarizes the framework we have set up, showing its major elements. The framework applies to our own perspectives on the question, and perspectives held by others.

FRAMEWORK OF ANALYSIS

ELEMENTS FOR
ANALYSIS

TIME	The three-dimensional character of an issue relative to past, present, and future
SOURCES	The style and commitments of individual and institutional sources
INFORMATION AND ANALYSIS	The theoretical perspectives The related factors relevant to analysis The range of factors and subjects used in analysis
CULTURAL FACTORS	The implicit value suppositions present in empirical analysis The beliefs and values appealed to for justification of behavior
BOUNDARIES OF MORAL CONCERN	The inclusiveness or exclusiveness of our moral concern

THE GLOBAL CRISIS

2

We have presupposed that there is a population crisis. Not all would agree, however, with that supposition nor would those who do agree share the same perspectives on the meaning and significance of the problem. Is there a problem at all? If so, whom does it include? How does the problem affect us? What are its potential consequences? Response to these questions can be grouped in four general categories.

First, many people are *unaware or unconcerned* about a population problem. They are the *disinterested*. This category includes people from both underdeveloped and developed nations, and it is the largest of the groups. One commentator observes that "Eighty to ninety percent of the world's people . . . know nothing about birth control."[1]

The second group says that *there is no population*

crisis.[2] This group includes some revolutionaries of the Third World, some writers of the New Left, and some officials in the Roman Catholic church. The revolutionaries maintain that the population explosion is a device invented by the Western world to keep the Third World down. Some insist that it is another racist ploy of whites attempting to decrease the number of non-whites. Several American black militants have charged that family planning is genocide. Roman Catholic writers have argued that the population crisis hides the need to find new food supply sources and social reform. The papal announcement on population carried this emphasis, although the statement does acknowledge a population problem.

These arguments might well be charged with having their own ideological blinders, preventing an adequate analysis of the situation, but they do make an important point when they say that population control is not a panacea. It won't solve every problem related to population.

The third approach is acknowledgement of a *population crisis in the world,* but this acknowledgement is limited to specific countries, or groups of people. There is a population crisis, but only in the Third World or among poorer peoples of the world.

The fourth approach, and the position that we will present in this chapter, says that there is a *world population crisis.* The population explosion confronts not only the Third World, but all of us—every nation in the world. It is not a local problem—it is a global crisis. Nations depend on each other. Because we are tied together in the world, we are in it together, sharing the problem.

The differences between group three and group four are crucial. Most Americans are in the third camp, and that approach is strong in its orientation towards particular situations. Some countries face a threat of massive starvation. Others are forced to stand still, even though economic development occurs. The weakness of this approach comes when analysis fails to move beyond the particular situation of a country to a global understanding. Nations do not exist by themselves—they are interrelated. The tendency, however, is to ignore the problem's global nature.

THE BOUNDARIES OF CONCERN

One reason a global perspective is difficult to accept is that nations, like people, tend to limit the boundaries of their action in terms of their own personal or national self-interest. Political philosophers such as Hans Morgenthau and Reinhold Niebuhr have long insisted that self-interest is a determining factor in social policy.[3] Thus a country that is underpopulated may well choose to emphasize a need for larger families, in spite of world population problems. In that way a country limits its consideration to the immediate demands of nationalistic self-interest.

A global perspective does not deny this condition nor does it deny self-interest as an inevitable dimension of politics. Rather it assumes that what is in the best interest of the world is in the best interest of individual nations. Using this perspective, an underpopulated country might emphasize immigration rather than large families, as a possible means of growth. America developed this way. Canada and Australia are still using this approach.

Let us look at four stances on the population problem and how they are related to the *interest* factor. They suggest the logical direction we would see nations taking as they move toward the global perspective and a stance of international self-interest.

The position of *disinterest* is a failure to recognize the problem. The significance of those who hold this position becomes frightening when we realize that only 20% of the people in Africa and 15% in Latin America are served by birth control programs.[4]

In the second stance of *national self-interest,* a nation is for or against policies of birth control in light of how it affects its immediate interests. International consequences are ignored.

The third stance is *interest in other specific countries.* Here a nation acts to aid another nation caught in a population dilemma. This is the situation we find today

39

where both voluntary and governmental agencies from such nations as the United States, Britain, and Japan attempt to provide population control assistance to other societies.

The fourth stance is *global*, involving *international self-interest* in which the problem is seen in a world perspective and the world's need becomes a primary concern in defining national self-interest. This movement from the first, second, or third stages to the fourth is not simple. It implies an extension of the *boundaries of concern*. This shift can be seen in very broad terms as a movement from a nationalistically oriented world to a world community. At best, we are somewhere "in between" in the shift. Reinhold Niebuhr has written of our dilemma:

> We are living in an age between the ages in which children are coming to birth but there is not strength to bring forth. We can see clearly what ought to be done to bring order and peace into the lives of the nations; but we do not have the strength to do what we ought. In fact this generation of mankind is destined to live in a tragic era when "one age is dead and the other is powerless to be born." [5]

He goes on to state that we see this image in our transition from a nationalistically oriented world to an understanding of the world as a global community.

> The age of absolute national sovereignty is over; but the age of international order under political instruments, powerful enough to regulate the relations of nations and to compose their competing desires, is not yet born.[6]

It may well be that the shift to a world community is possible only through a step by step recognition of our interdependence around such problems as population. It already occurs in embryonic fashion with such issues as monetary policy where, for example, nations realize that devaluation of currency in one country affects other countries and therefore all must be concerned. For this to occur around the issue of population, it is necessary for empirical evidence to show that population is a world issue and affects the interest of us all. It seems to me that evidence bears this out if it is weighed carefully and extensively. Two tendencies in population analysis, however, have limited our seeing this. One has been the tendency to limit the examination to a country's immediate situation. In the process an orientation to the present has dominated the analysis. For example, it is possible to say that Ethiopia has no problems since her birth rate is balanced by her death rate. This ignores the fact that Ethiopia is a developing country which will probably experience a decreasing death rate as health conditions are improved. And it ignores the historical attitudes and norms which will make it difficult for Ethiopia to respond to a rising birth rate with extensive population control programs.

A second tendency has been the failure to acknowledge the *world wide implications* of certain factors which are affected by population increase.

One of these factors is economic. The chart on page 28 shows that poor nations are faced with the highest birth rates. These nations want to develop, but even though they make economic strides their birth rate is so high that capital needed for further investment and expansion is wiped out. Robert McNamara, President of the World Bank, summarized the situation when he noted in his now famous speech on population that:

> Current birth rates throughout the emerging world are seriously crippling developmental efforts. It is imperative to understand why. The intractable reason is that these governments must divert an inordinately high proportion of their limited national savings away from productive investment simply in order to maintain the current low level of existence.[7]

It could be assumed that this does not affect economically developed countries with lower birth rates. But when we see the growing gap between the have and have-not nations, the problem takes on world wide significance. In world economics, the weakest link determines the strength of the whole. We are bound together so tightly that the condition of one nation necessarily affects the condition of others.

This interrelatedness is not limited to economics but also includes the political dimension. War has been the traditional solution to overpopulation. Not only does it reduce population, but it also offers the possibility of more land to provide food and resources. The situation today is potentially explosive. Overpopulated China is next door to underpopulated Russia. Overpopulated South Asia is next to sparsely populated Australia. A dangerously increasing Latin American population grows next door to North America. These are strong reminders that the momentary luxury enjoyed by wealthier nations may be fleeting, if population growth and control is not seen in a world perspective.

The ecological factor is also crucial. The interdependence of people and nature has received extensive treatment recently. Man has his place in the environment, and its boundaries must be observed. If they are not, the balance of nature may be destroyed, destroying the possibility of human life in the process. Man may use the natural resources available, but when his exploitation goes beyond certain limits a chain of reactions is set off against him. Recent discussions of air and water pollution show that this possibility is not far-fetched. A 1968 UNESCO report suggests that we have 20 years before "the planet starts becoming uninhabitable because of air pollution." [8] The effects of chemical pesticides like DDT can be traced from ponds in Minnesota to ocean life, and back again to the milk of Minnesota mothers. Already the DDT intake of infants is twice as high as the allowable maximum set by the World Health Organization, and its use is world wide. Wayne Davis, a biologist, writes about the use of DDT in underdeveloped nations:

> Since DDT is the cheapest and these nations the poorest, that pesticide will be used. Yet it is common knowledge that DDT adversely affects species in the various links of the marine food chain from algae to fish and birds. New and more drastic effects are seen each year. DDT is the probable cause of the collapse of the herring fisher of the North Sea where Iceland's major industry has fallen by more than 90 percent since 1966. It is likely involved in the decline of our

*haddock landings from 50,000 tons in 1964 to 20,000
in 1969 due to spawning failures*

*As little as 10 parts per billion of DDT in ocean water
inhibits photosynthesis in marine algae. Not only are
algae the base of the food chain upon which all other
marine life depend, but they also produce 70 to 90
percent of the world's oxygen.*[9]

The picture is further complicated by the short supply
of many of our natural resources, compounded by the
greater demands of an increasing population. Shortages
of fuels like coal and oil have already been forecast.
Even more significant, however, is the increasingly serious food shortage. Strides are being made in food increases through the development of better strains of
grain, increased use of fertilizer and pesticides, and
better land management. In the so-called "green revolution," for example, we have seen the emergence of
new strains of rice, IR-8. Wheat, corn, and sorghum are
also being improved. Lester Brown, Administrator of the
U.S.D.A.'s Foreign Agricultural Service was quoted in
the *Population Chronicle:*

> *The new varieties are much more responsive to fer-
> tilizer than traditional varieties. Under proper growing
> conditions, they out-yield traditional varieties not by
> a mere 10, 20, or 30 percent but by a multiple of two
> or more. This is why they have caught the imagination
> of so many Asian farmers.*

He goes on to add:

> *. . . far more than the old rice, IR-8 is responsive to
> scientific farm management, to far heavier doses of
> fertilizer, to timely pesticide treatment, to a broad
> range of improved practices. Not only do farmers
> learn through experience that the so-called "miracle
> rice" works; they learn that it works better if accom-
> panied by generally improved production technology.*[10]

In spite of these improvements, however, the situation
still stands at the crisis point due to the improved
strains increasing dependence on pesticides which
compound the problem, and the simple fact that we

come nowhere near providing an adequate food supply even with these improvements.[11]

B. R. Sen, former Director General of the Food and Agricultural Organization of the United Nations has noted:

Sixty-three million people are being added every year to the world population, and the increase is taking place at a higher rate in the poorer countries of Asia, Africa and Latin America than in the more advanced and prosperous parts of Europe and North America. On the other hand, food production is not keeping pace with the growth of population. In 1963-64 according to FAC's "The State of Food and Agriculture 1964," farm production rose by between 1 and 2 percent, appreciably less than the growth of population. FCO indices show no gain at all in food production per head since 1958-59, while in three of the developing regions, Africa, Latin America and the Far East, food production per head has tended to decline over the past few years . . .[12]

It is not just a question of the quantity of consumption but also the quality. There is a sharp difference between the have and the have-not nations of the world. People in the have nations consume 50 grams of protein and a 1000 more calories per day. People in the have-not nations consume 10 grams of protein per day with much greater dependency on cereals and starches.[13]

Against this background, a note written by Sen in 1965 takes on ominous significance:

I may repeat what I have said elsewhere, that unless drastic measures are taken to raise agricultural productivity, the present precarious balance between population growth and food production will break down and large-scale famines, which may prove beyond control, will begin to appear in some parts of the world before 1980.[14]

Some analysts are predicting such famines for the late 1970s.

There are over 3¹/₂ billion people in the world today. It is estimated that up to half are starving and 10 to 15%

44

more are undernourished. There may be resources to keep all the population at a subsistence level *but such a distribution does not exist nor will it occur.* Presently, the West consumes 80% of the resources of the world for its own use.[15] Given that condition, one wonders where the claims of justice are to be heard. If we choose to look at this in global terms we see that our own consumption is at the expense of human life elsewhere.

The peoples of the West may have a lower birth rate but their consumption is many times greater than that of other nations. When we speak of the effect of over-population on the world in relation to resource drain, technological pollution, and other problems, we have to realize that one person in our own population is equivalent to hundreds in some countries and thousands in others. Consequently, the wealthy nations are equally guilty of overpopulation

The global implications of these political, economic, and ecological factors are often ignored. When they are ignored it is easy to conclude that the population problem is limited to certain countries or regions. That, however, is a false picture. Population is a world problem—it affects us all.

Perhaps Niebuhr's statement that we "live in an age between the ages" best defines our dilemma. We can see the need for recognizing the moral claims of the world community as a whole, but we do not do it.

But before this can be recognized those beliefs and values which inform a society to be more inclusive—to view life in a world wide framework of mutual interdependence and need—must be given a priority in new and powerful images that can change the perspectives that shape our present limited response. Such values are present in the residue of good will that directs a nation to respond to other nations in moments of catastrophe. After the 1970 earthquakes in Peru, for example, several nations joined hands to help people of that nation. In our own society, we have developed the mechanisms for responding to disasters throughout the country so that the nation as a whole may come to the rescue of a region, area, or group.

There must be a reordering of cultural values so that they become inclusive, affirm our interdependence, and sanction a sense of oneness with the world and its ills.

Certainly Christianity includes the imperative to see all structures in finite terms in which each can legitimately make its claim. Furthermore, the inclusive thrust implied in the moral imperatives of love and justice provides a further base for morally recognizing and legitimating a global perspective.

Other factors could be given as limiting our scope in approaching the population issue. Hopefully, in exploring these, we have outlined the case for accepting the global perspective as the necessary point of departure. If we view the above factors in terms of their constructive support of a global perspective, we can insist that the following approach be followed.

1. The analysis of the problem as it is related to any entity, individual or international, must take into consideration not only the short range present situation but also the implications of both the past and the future—how historical forces do and will impinge upon a continuing response to the issue and what the long range projections for the world situations suggest. In effect, what the future will look like insofar as we can predict it.

Let us be quick to say that the recognition of the issue's three dimensional character will not necessarily lead to a position in which international interest becomes a primary concern. What I am suggesting is that its recognition contributes to an awareness of the issue's global nature by introducing a broader perspective on the question.

2. The recognition of economic, political, ecological, and other factors not only in terms of their specific meaning for individual countries but within their world wide context. This means, however, that we are always ready to ask the question, "What is the situation in global terms?" as well as "What is the situation in terms of a given country?"

3. The third area of change is to extend our own moral boundaries so that our approach shifts from an exclusive

to an inclusive ethical perspective. This means that we will need to reinterpret our own beliefs and values in such a fashion that they invite consideration of the population problem in its global as well as in its more narrowed terms.

In suggesting this fundamental shift to a global frame, we are not suggesting that nations cease to consider their own unique situations nor that they in some naive fashion be expected to ignore their own national self-interest. What is suggested is that national self-interest be defined in light of the world wide situation. It is a matter of realizing that we are all on the same space ship, as Kenneth Boulding has suggested, and that if one sector of the world's travelers, for whatever reason, start us on a trek to oblivion, we all will share that journey's destiny.

THE CRISIS IN THE UNITED STATES

3

Two basic questions concern us.

First, does the United States of America have a population problem? We will argue that it has a problem within its own borders and that this problem expresses itself as a unique dimension of the global crisis.

Second, does the United States actually see itself as a part of the global problem? The answer is no. Though the United States has shown concern for the population problems of particular nations, it has not yet identified itself as a part of the dilemma. It has not yet moved to a position of international concern and acceptance of the problem.

The American fertility rate has been declining since 1957 though that decline has now ceased. (The fertility rate is the rate of births per 1000 women in the child-bearing range (15-44), while the birth rate refers to the number of births per 1000 people). If we trace the fer-

49

tility growth rate from its lowest point during the depression of the early 1930's, we find this cycle:[1]

		123		
		(1957)		
	106		119	
	(1950)		(1960)	
80				98
(1940)				(1965)
75.8				85.7
(1936)				(1968)
(all time low)				

To appreciate what this cycle means we need to note first that it represents an increase beyond simple replacement (zero population growth). As one analysis suggests:

> Had the 1936 fertility rate of 75.8 been maintained, it would have led to an approximately stationary population. A fertility rate of 85, if maintained and if current rates of death, sterility, and sexual union continue, would lead to an increase in population. Such a fertility rate, continued over the full thirty-year period of fertility, would result in a total of 2,550 live births per thousand women, representing a completed family of 2.55 children per woman. Taking into account current rates of death, sterility, and sexual union, only 2.1 children per woman are needed to insure a stationary population. The difference between 2.5 and 2.1 represents an excess fertility of approximately 20 percent above replacement level.[2]

Though the baby boom peaked in 1957, the subsequent decline reached its low in 1968 and we are now seeing an increase. Whether the upward movement will continue depends on what the children of the baby boom decide about their own family size. They are just entering the childbearing period.[3]

Finally, we should recognize that our population, now over 200 million, may reach 300 million by the year 2000.

This means that we will have an even greater potential for growth—a growth rate increases the number of potential mothers. It takes more time to reproduce the first million than it does to reproduce the next million.

But fertility growth rates and their trends provide only statistical data. To understand what the numbers mean, we have to turn to the significance of population growth for certain sectors of the society. In this discussion we will point to three different positions held in the present debate over the meaning of population growth in America.

The first position sees the population dilemma as a global crisis and increased population control as a sufficient means for solving the major issues of our day. The second position also assumes the global nature of the problem but insists that such control, though a necessary means to the solution of major problems, is not sufficient in and of itself. The third position insists that the population crisis is real but essentially located in other parts of the world. In turn, it maintains that for America, population growth, not control, is needed to battle the problems we face in our own society and the world at large.

The *first position* is the most extreme and reductionistic. It assumes that population control is the key to solving the full range of ecological, social, and economic problems of our age. To those who take this stance, the failure of government, private groups, and individuals to give adequate attention to the problem spells doom for us as a nation and as a world. For them the problem is a growth cycle which overloads the natural environment, the economy, housing, educational institutions, recreational areas, and welfare programs. The cycle can be broken only if we stop the primary input—people.

The argument is not new. Margaret Sanger, the *grande dame* of the birth control movement, saw the sexual drive as the central force in humanity. She claimed that the moral, psychological, economic, and social health of the nation depended upon an adequate control of its procreative dimension. Its control, she insisted, was the key to the maintenance of civilization.

This orientation can be shared by strange bedfellows. It may include an industrialist who wants the pollution monkey off his back and finds an easy out in the statistical abstractions of birth rate fluctuations. It can equally include the conservationist who again and again in seeking a way out of the environmental crisis is confronted by the overwhelming implications of population growth.

The problem with this argument, as Third World revolutionaries have insisted, is that it oversimplifies the world's ills. It is reductionistic. It reduces the cause of our ills to one primary source and its solutions to one basic response. The high birth rate is the demon; salvation is its control. The problem is that the crises of our natural and social environments are not simply the products of population size. This factor is only contributory, even if it is crucial. Poverty, for example, may not be eliminated without extensive and efficient fertility control; but after such control becomes a reality, poverty will still remain unless other causes are also dealt with.

The second position, which we will maintain, acknowledges the United States is a part of a global crisis; an increased check on our population growth rate is essential in responding if the issues plagueing us are to be solved. But, as we have suggested, it does not assume that control will be the panacea for our ills. It is rather one necessary condition that must be met. The United States does have a problem unique to its own situation and this problem coupled with its own interrelatedness to the rest of the world makes it a part of the global crisis. The problem, moreover, must be seen in its interrelatedness to a range of factors, including the economy, technology, natural resources, and the spatial and social spheres.

According to the third position, a position held by many traditional economists, population growth is necessary. The major argument is that as population grows, more taxable income should become available. The new taxes, in turn, would enable us to fight the problems facing us. Its equation is simple. Population growth equals a growing economy which means new resources to deal with unresolved problems. One advocate of this argument, Ben Wattenberg, states in response to the assumption that more people means more pollution:

> Population is one of the variables in the pollution problem. Yet there is something else to be said. People not only cause pollution, but once you have a substantial number of people, it is only people that can stop pollution. Further, the case can be made that more people can more easily and quickly solve pollution problems than can fewer people.

He goes on to argue that this is the case primarily because there is basically

> one time capital costs of research that must go into any effective, long range, anti-pollution problem. The costs are roughly the same for 200 or 300 million people—but easier to pay by 300 million.[4]

Herman Miller, head of the Population Division of the United States Census Bureau and a demographer, argues a similar case by insisting that it takes people to generate the economy.[5] Both Wattenberg and Miller are responsive to the dangers of population growth and Miller acknowledges that there will come a time when growth will have to stop. But neither is overly concerned at the moment. Wattenberg is even nonchalant about the issue.

> Certainly, too, population growth must sooner or later level off. While America could support twice its current population and probably four times its current population—growth can obviously not go on forever and it is wise to understand this fact now rather than a hundred years from now. It is also wise to begin to act upon this knowledge as indeed we have begun to act upon it. . . . Our problem in the future will probably be easier to handle with somewhat fewer people than with somewhat greater numbers.[6]

The major difficulty with the third position's argument is its failure to recognize that the problems will grow as a consequence of population growth, making them even more difficult to solve. For even if the economy and subsequently tax revenues do grow, more people will mean

53

greater problems and more expensive solutions. It may be, as Wattenberg argues, that the capital cost for research is not higher for an increased population. But the same is not true for the *actual cost* of eliminating the problem. For, though basic research costs may remain relatively fixed, the cost of the production and programming necessary for the problem's solution will increase. We may have more money to deal with pollution, but pollution will be more extensive, programs will have to be larger, and implementation will inevitably be more costly, particularly if our present form and direction of economic expansion continues.

Furthermore, many problems caused by population increase require little cost in terms of research, but major expenditures at the point of implementation. Expanding facilities and programs for housing, schools, and recreational areas is expensive.

The argument also ignores that a reordering of priorities is the most logical way to release funds for research and action. That coupled with a zero population growth rate represents a far more sane program than unchecked increases in population and economic growth.

Underlying the difference between the second and third positions is also a basically different understanding of the significance of economic growth. For the position we have been attacking is essentially committed to economic growth as a given process which must be maintained. Thus other issues are to be adjusted to facilitate that process, whether it is the problem of population or pollution. Hendrick Houthakker, a member of the President's Council of Economic Advisers, in defending this notion against the ecologists, writes:

> *It may seem old fashioned, indeed reactionary, to emphasize the growth of output as the first objective of economic policy. . . . It is now fashionable to stress the deleterious effects of growth, especially on the environment and some wits have gone so far as to say that GNP means Gross National Pollution. The notion of further growth conjures up visions of more cars, more highways, more pesticides, and more of many other things that are not as popular as they used to be.*[7]

In our own position, however, we would insist that though we must weigh the effect of population control on the economy, we must equally weigh its effect on other spheres of life. Economic growth, and particularly specific directions and types of growth, should be subjected to questions and control if its effects on other spheres is negative.[8]

Life is not exclusively economic. Other factors are involved and they must be held in balance in decision making. Here we will look at the effect of population growth on some of these other sectors.

POPULATION GROWTH AND RESOURCES

Both coal and oil—in broader terms, fossil fuels—are being depleted and may be used up in thirty to fifty years. These fuels are essential for developing and maintaining an industrial world. At the present time a major search for a replacement fuel is underway. The sooner a replacement is found the better, since coal and oil are major pollutants.

The popular and optimistic answer to the dilemma of depletion and pollution is nuclear power. Wattenburg takes this approach in suggesting that "whether ore reserves are depleted in 2020 or 2040 or 2140 does not seem to be of crucial importance; in any event, a substitute must be found—probably nuclear."[9] But it isn't that simple. As population ecologist Wayne Davis notes in referring to the conclusion of Sheldon Novick's book *The Careless Atom*, ". . . the rush to more and even larger nuclear reactors may be the most ecologically insane thing we've come up with yet."[10] Nuclear power solves neither pollution nor the depletion problem. A congressional subcommittee, headed by Representative Enrilio Daddario, reported that

> There has been little progress in devising a way to get rid of the toxic by-products (of the nuclear power plants). The best we can do with radio-active waste is what we first thought of—bury it. But someday that system will no longer be possible. Then what? At this point there is no convincing evidence that anyone really knows.[11]

55

A thin margin of time may be our most valuable ally. Population control can contribute to that margin by cutting both depletion and pollution.

POPULATION GROWTH AND SPACE

It is often pointed out that the United States has an abundance of space and could support a much larger population. This is a favorite argument of the growth proponents. It could be called the North Dakota solution. Some states like North Dakota are losing population. When this is coupled with an already small population, it makes a wealth of space available for growth. Supporters of this position also claim that in comparison with countries like Holland and England, the United States is sparsely settled. We therefore have nothing to fear.

When we examine the space argument with more care, however, the scene is not so picturesquely simple. For the real question is not the quantity of space but its locale, quality, and relationship to other spheres of the social system. The issue can be explained by referring to the population *implosion,* a sharp population increase in areas that are already densely populated. In a technological society population movement is dependent on the presence of sophisticated economic, social, political, and cultural support systems. Such systems exist in the urban areas but not in areas that are sparsely settled. These areas could be developed. The "New Town" idea includes the notion of creating such communities from the ground up. But "New Towns" and artificial pump priming of depressed areas is expensive, complex, and by no means a ready solution to population distribution.

Both geographical and socioeconomic factors dictate that growth will occur in areas that are already heavily populated. Population growth is not evenly distributed, nor will it be; areas strained now will be even more overloaded in the future. This does not deny either the possibility or the desirability of growth in presently underpopulated areas. But more is required than moving chrome-lined trailers to the middle of the Great Plains.[12]

Population control will not solve the question of over-crowded urban areas nor will it lead to decentralization and redistribution. But it is one factor in curbing crowding and it is a positive means of complementing programs to deal with such a condition.

Perhaps most significant, however, is the simple fact that Americans consume space as if it were infinite. We have never had to conserve space or face to any great degree the negative effects of high density situations. Consequently our situation is not analogous with the Netherlands. We do not have the Hollander's sophistication in dealing with the phenomenon of high density, or the value system that sustains it. We can change, but that has yet to take place. The space issue is more complex than the North Dakota argument allows.

POPULATION GROWTH AND SOCIAL ISSUES

Many population alarmists see control as *the basic way* of solving fundamental social problems. Put in those terms the argument is unacceptable. It ignores the crucial role of structures and their need for reorganization and development in the process of solving social problems. At the same time, however, population makes a significant contribution to social problems.

For example, the fertility rate is greater in the poorer classes and it is a contributing factor to the poverty cycle. Control of family size among the poor will not catapult them into the affluent classes—large family size is only one of many causal factors related to poverty. Nevertheless, control is a crucial need in dealing with poverty.

It should be acknowledged that such control is not easy to achieve among the poor, for large families are often seen as desirable. Judith Blake points to the dilemma in an article in *Science*:

> The data lend little support to the hypothesis that the poor desire families as small as those desired by the middle and upper classes. Within both the educational and the economic categories, those on the lower rungs not only have larger families than those on the higher rungs (at least in the case of non-Catholics) but they

57

say they want larger families and consider them ideal. This differential has existed for as long as information on preferred family size in this country has been available, and it persists.[13]

This fact, however, simply bears out the need for more extensive and diverse control programs that can shift the image of desirable family size.

To change the focus, it should also be pointed out that the affluent often dismiss the need to limit fertility on the basis that they can afford a large family. For the American, particularly, this argument is justification enough. What the argument ignores, however, is the disproportionate consumption of a large affluent family —a point to be explored in more detail later.

An explosive emotional issue related to the race issue emerges here. Many black militants have argued that birth control for the black is an attempt to check a growing minority when it is gaining power. This argument is naive at best, and fallacious at worst. Minority power, and specifically black power in this society at this point in history, is dependent not on numbers but on strategies and the sophisticated use of pressure. Discrimination against minorities is not because of numbers. Rather it is a result of cultural, institutional racism. As Heer has noted

the American Negroes are most persecuted where they form the largest proportion of the population. From the standpoint of civil rights, the relative position of the American Negro is at its worst in Mississippi, Alabama, and the other Deep South states wherein Negroes form a relatively large proportion of the total population and at its best in those Northern and Western states with relatively small Negro populations....[14]

If anything, population control aids in the struggle by releasing economic, psychological, and social energies and resources from childcare for political and social organization and action. At this point in the struggle this is crucial.

Finally, the growing pressure for better education, medical attention, social recreation, and housing is complicated by an increasing population. Again, population control will not solve these problems, but it is a significant variable in their solution.

THE UNITED STATES AND THE WORLD CRISIS

The most sobering dimension of the population issue is the relationship of the American situation to the rest of the world. Examining it from a global perspective forces us to see the depths of the crisis. The United States is technologically the most developed nation in the world and a demanding consumer. This consumption, created by the technology, feeds the world's population crisis.[15] To appreciate this let us look at the American as technological man.

Every American expects access to our nation's technological advantages. But technology comes at a price. Every use of an invention like the internal combustion engine, the electric can opener, the garbage disposal, or the plastic bag requires the use of resources and power that leave their mark on the social and physical environment. The following list represents a part of what we throw away in a year:

90 million tons of auto pollutants
142 million tons of smoke and fumes
7 million junked cars
20 million tons of waste paper
48 billion used cans
50 trillion gallons of industrial sewage
32 billion used glass bottles
100 million worn out tires
15,600 pieces of litter per highway mile[16]

In the first phase of his consumption cycle the newborn American is quickly socialized to expect the fruits of technology. He is created in the image of a mythical figure called "the great consumer," and in the finest tradition of naive piety he emulates the master with little deviance from its demands. In the second part of the cycle, the economy itself is geared to help socialize him

59

and meet his continuing thirst and desire for consumption. As an economy it works under a fundamental law of production—"if it will sell, produce it." In turn, the mass media, serving as the handmaiden of mass advertising, orient their powers toward convincing the potential consumer that consumption is good and an unquestioned right. In this process the soft and the hard, the subtle and the gross demands to consume the fruits of technology go on without any reference to implications for resource depletion, power pollution or social costs. The presupposition is that whatever technology produces, man is to consume. Anyone who questions that presupposition is reassured that it is both economically justifiable and necessary by that most intriguing of technological creations, the Madison Avenue drawing board. We thus become the servants of technology.

In the process, the technological spiraling continues like a tennis match which reaches deuce only to have an add-in, then a return to deuce, then an add-out and again a return to deuce with the actual production and consumption increasing like the length of the game, the environment feeling the strain, like the players, with no end in sight.

If this process occurred within our own borders, affecting only our destiny, its relationship to the world's population would be minimal. But it does not. It directly increases the crisis because it needs the world's resources to feed its technological development. Thus the American becomes, as the wealthy consumer of technological production, an enormously expensive sub-species consuming far beyond his share of the world's goods. Paul Ehrlich summarizes the situation when he writes:

> We, of course, cannot remain affluent and isolated. At the moment the United States uses well over half of all the raw materials consumed each year. Think of it. Less than 1/15 of the population of the world requires more than all the rest to maintain its inflated position. If present trends continue, in 20 years we will get much less than 1/15th of the population, and yet we may use some 80% of the resources consumed. Our affluence depends heavily on many different kinds

of imports: ferroalloys (metals used to make various kinds of steel), tin, bauxite (aluminum ore), rubber, and so forth. Will other countries, many of them in the grip of starvation and anarchy, still happily supply these materials to a nation that cannot give them food? Even the technological optimists don't think we can free ourselves of the need for imports in the near future, so we're going to be up against it.[17]

The fact that we consume 70% of the world's proteins is even more devastating, especially when it is combined with another fact—protein deficiency during pregnancy directly affects the mental potential of the child. Thus we make our own contribution to the limitation and destruction of life in other parts of the world, even before birth.

When we step back from these arguments and assess their implications for American society and the world, we see a striking chord running through them all: the quality of life, both environmental and social, will be negatively affected if the birth rate is not controlled. At some points the effect will be gradual—at other points, dramatic. If the present trends continue, however, no aspect of life will escape. Birth control is not a magic solution to every problem that we face as a nation or as a world. But no solution is possible without it. A zero growth rate, therefore, is a necessary ingredient in any attempt to act effectively.

Looking at the population problem from a global perspective—looking at the American problem—the conclusion is inescapable: population growth threatens our survival. Effective action must be forthcoming.

The empirical verification of the crisis as global, and the United States' participation in it, does not necessarily mean that we accept this situation ideologically or politically. When we look at our own world and national policies, it becomes apparent that we have neither recognized nor accepted it. We have no comprehensive international or domestic policies on population problems. It is a low priority item at home and abroad.

In light of this fact our discussion turns to an examination of certain values and beliefs that contribute to our failure to respond. We shall turn to an examination of the role overarching myths and belief patterns play as they inform our conceptualization of the issue. We will argue that individuals and the society as a whole must change basic attitudes if we are to recognize, accept, and respond to the crisis.

VALUES AND CRISIS: THE INDIVIDUAL

4

In the last two chapters we have argued that the United States is part of the world population crisis. The dilemma is that the United States does not really accept her part in the crisis. What must happen for such acceptance to take place?

In this chapter and the next, we will argue that we need a basic change in the cultural paradigms through which we interpret the meaning of procreation and the population crisis. Since the categories "paradigm" and "culture" are central to our discussion, let us begin with a definition of each.

A paradigm is a perspective or theory through which we see and interpret reality. It orders beliefs, attitudes, and facts to give reality a particular shape and meaning. For example, if a person were to tell us that procreation is a process of nature which has been ordained by God as the primary purpose of sex and should not in any fashion be thwarted by contraception, he would be showing us the paradigm through which he understands the meaning and signficance of procreation. He has ordered his understanding of God, nature, and sex in a particular fashion. If he also takes seriously the population explosion and its implications for extensive birth control programs, he may find that his paradigm does not allow him to realistically interpret and respond to the problem. He may find, therefore, that his perspective must shift or change.[1]

The term "cultural" refers to a belief system that includes the symbols, myths, values, and norms held by a given people or society.[2] The controlling set of symbols is religious, expressing what Paul Tillich called man's ultimate concern. Religious values are normative concepts that define what is desirable in interpreting the ultimate meaning of human existence. Values which inform our understanding of fertility control include individualism and our view of nature.

The first paradigm is related to an individual approach to procreation and its control. It tells us that family size must be controlled, but it also maintains that a family is *necessary* to human fulfillment. Furthermore, it assumes that family size is determined only by the individual's immediate situation.

The second paradigm concerns our relationship as a nation to our own population situation and the world crisis. It calls us to a faith in technology and growth which, coupled with an image of ourselves as a chosen people, allows us to assume that we need not fear a national crisis or identify ourselves as part of a world crisis.

Both paradigms are inadequate. They distort our perspective and our response, extending an invitation to eventual global disaster.

The first paradigm with its understanding of procreation and control is the perspective that informs most Americans. At its root are important theological and cultural presuppositions about nature that inform our receptivity to population control. It is with this view of nature that we begin our discussion.

The second paradigm will be taken up in the next chapter. In both cases, we will also explore some possibilities for a new and more accurate paradigm. We should acknowledge, however, that new approaches are not easily determined, nor are they predictable. They do not come from planning boards, but rather emerge through the understandings and imaginations of society as a whole.

CONTROL OF NATURE

A major dimension of a society's orientation toward reality is conceptualized in its *view of nature* and the fashion in which nature is to be controlled. This view is obviously important here since birth control affects a fundamental natural process.

Attitudes towards nature differ from culture to culture. Certain American Indian tribes, for example, saw themselves achieving a harmony with nature. European invaders, however, brought a sharply different view which was to form the basis of our own perspective.

Max Weber, a German sociologist of the turn of the century, provides insight into this Western perspective in his sociological examination of Reformation Protestantism and particularly Calvinism.[8] He observed that Calvinist piety maintained certain overarching beliefs that had a "pragmatic" significance for human behavior. The heart of this piety was belief in a sovereign and transcendent God who ruled over a creation that was finite and subject to his will. Man was ordained to give glory to God through obedience to his divine will—a will revealed in divine law and the natural order of the universe. This gave rise to what Weber called a "this-worldly asceticism," "an active ascetic response to all spheres of life." This asceticism was ethically oriented: obedience expressed itself in an active ethical control of all reality in the interest of serving God. The emphasis on *control* was central. A person's work, for example, was not just a way to make a living; it was to be controlled, like all reality, to give God glory. All that was "secular" had a sacred dimension insofar as it could be used by man in God's service. In turn, nothing was intrinsically sacred for the sacral quality depended on the nature of its use.

The natural order, though respected as the creation of God, had no sacral properties. Like other realms, it was to be studied and responded to in terms of how it might serve the purposes of God's will. Consequently, it was subject to man's manipulation and control. For our immediate concern, this emphasis on manipulation and control is crucial.

Sexuality came into this understanding at two levels. Since sex was considered a peculiarly powerful enticement, rational self-conscious control was emphasized. This did not make it intrinsically evil. Intention determined whether the act was right or wrong. Sexual intimacy, shared in moderation with one's wife, could be viewed as a part of the mutual companionship husband and wife were called to share. Procreation was the blessing of that relationship, ordained by God for the replenishment of the human race.

Parenthood carried with it responsibilities for adequate nurture and moral education. The child was to be socialized to respond in ethical obedience to the will of God.

It is a long journey from John Calvin and the Calvinist to contemporary society. The emphases that have been stressed, however, became part of English Puritanism, left their impact on the aggressive sect groups of England, and came with the *Mayflower* as cultural seeds that were to take deep root in the American soil. In the process, this view of man in relationship to nature was internalized within the cultural system of America.

The influence of the Calvinistic approach on American Protestantism contributed to its receptivity to birth control. In the 19th century, many Americans with their Victorian fears of sexual pleasure, attacked contraception because it provided a means for unrestrained and hence uncontrolled sexual indulgence. At the same time, however, there was concern for controlling fertility so that it would serve the primary purposes God had ordained for the world. Furthermore, in the 19th century, this approach essentially expressed the dominant American

66

cultural perspective. The basic orientation of this period was that conception should be planned and controlled or rationalized to accord with given needs, ends, or purposes beyond the act itself. This is the controlling motif of family planning—that children should be planned in terms of specific concerns that are acknowledged and weighed in the decision-making process.[4]

This understanding of control has been studied by population analysts. It has been seen as one key to the West's acceptance of family planning. It has been further suggested that a cultural equivalent to this approach may well be necessary for the acceptance of birth control in underdeveloped countries where birth rates remain rampant.

The problem in the American situation today is that, since we are favorably predisposed to practice birth control, it is assumed that we *will* do so in accord with the needs of the time. It is when we make this assumption that a fundamental distortion occurs. For we presume that a willingness to control will *necessarily* lead to an adequate degree of control. In effect, our orientation towards nature legitimates the control of procreation and indicates that such control should be decided in a coherent and ordered fashion, but does not determine whether that control will be made in light of global, societal, family, or individual goals. Nor does it determine whether the control will be for a well-spaced but large family or for a small number of children. What we have to realize is that there are other value orientations which affect this dimension of the decision-making process and that those orientations must be dealt with if we are to achieve a more appropriate population growth rate. Two such orientations are those related to procreation and to individualism—the subjects of our remaining inquiry in understanding our paradigm.

PROCREATION

The value with which we must next deal involves *procreation* itself. In all previous civilizations and eras, the threat of underpopulation was greater than the threat of overpopulation. Infant mortality was high—uncontrollable plagues, wars, and natural disasters limited population growth. Under these conditions, procreation had a religious significance. It was grounded as a central value in all the great religious systems. The oft-quoted phrase "be fruitful and multiply" and the affirmation of a large family as a sign of success, symbolically spoken of by the writer of Psalm 127 as a "quiver full of arrows," are examples of a continuing motif in the Old Testament. There are equivalents in all cultural religious systems.

When we enter the modern age, overpopulation is the condition—a low fertility norm is needed. Yet a high fertility orientation persists. Thus people tragically continue to desire large families when the world desperately needs to check that desire.

In the United States, where the birth rate is not as high as in many countries, the tendency is to assume that the fertility norm is adequately circumscribed. This assumption may well blind us to two very important realities which can contribute to a higher than acceptable birth rate or make it difficult to bring the birth rate down to an acceptable level: zero population growth. The first is the degree to which our pro-fertility norm permeates the fabric of social roles, attitudes, and images of the ideal family. The second is the tendency to consider fertility control primarily in terms of individual needs and goals rather than societal, global, and ecological needs. The first of these conditions we will explore now; the second will be considered in the discussion of individualism.

In American society, procreation has been considered *necessary* for human fulfillment. A childless person is incomplete. Child-bearing is not just one avenue to fulfillment—it is an essential avenue. People don't justify having children—they justify not having them. Childless couples are questioned. One child families are asked about the next arrival. Adoption is seen as a second-best alternative.

Further, there is a latent affirmation of large families in American society, even though the average family now might be smaller than in previous generations. Television commercials, usually bellwether sources of safe and commonly held attitudes, hold the large family up for admiration, especially in the middle and upper classes. One especially clever cereal ad put a woman in the best of both worlds—a mother of six who looked like her oldest daughter.

A more striking example of this emphasis on fertility is the role ascribed to the American woman. A woman *must* have children to fulfill herself as a person. Meaning itself is dependent on bearing and nurturing a child. The woman may substitute a career or other involvements for motherhood, but if she does she is deviant; the system feels compelled to either sympathize with or discriminate against her. Even in sophisticated institutions such as the University of Minnesota, women's salaries—for the same job, of the same rank and experience—are less than men's.[5]

All this adds up to a very strong pro-fertility norm. Procreation is understandably a sacrosanct value in a society. It is the source of continued existence. The point is not that it has to be sacrificed; rather, it must be more adequately controlled. To achieve this control, the norms and values that influence family size need to be reexamined and challenged. This isn't easy. Given the problem, it is necessary.

INDIVIDUALISM

Perhaps no cultural value is so fundamentally rooted in the American psyche as individualism.[6] The parents of American ideology—European Protestantism and Enlightenment political philosophy—made this value central in their own belief systems. It was permanently embodied in the Bill of Rights as fundamental, and an elaborate mythology has borne this value to each generation. The symbols which carry its meaning are legion: the 1776 Minutemen, Natty Bumpo, the saved souls of Whitefield, Finney, and Cartwright, the canonized Lincolns, Kennedys, and Kings, and overarching them all, the cowboy and his domestic cousin, the frontiersman.

For the American, individualism legitimated certain inalienable rights more sacred that the nation itself. It made the subject of his attention the cultivation and satisfaction of his own needs and goals.[7]

Individualism has affected the understanding of procreation in two ways. First, it assured the individual's right to determine how many children he would have. Secondly, it focused on the individual as the primary, if not the only, subject for moral consideration in determining family size.

The deep-rootedness of the first expression is evident in the response of a college ethics seminar on the population problem. After a long session probing the various dimensions of the question and the possible role of government policy, the students were asked: do you think that the couple has the absolute right to determine family size regardless of the number desired? The response was definite: eleven insisted that in spite of population problems, any couple desiring a large family should have the right to have one.

Like all rights, this is limited by societal attitudes. We insist that it is exercised responsibly only if it occurs within wedlock and only if it takes into consideration the ability to adequately provide for the child's basic needs. Even here, however, the right is sacred enough that irresponsible procreation seldom justifies suspension of the right.

A second dimension of individualism's effect on procreation is the tendency to limit the definition to a consideration of the specific individuals involved, namely, the couple and the child. Thus, many factors may be considered in determining whether or not to have a child—economic, social, psychological—but these factors are limited to the individuals immediately involved. Thus, a couple insisting on a fourth child in an effort to conceive a son gives priority to its psychological and social needs. The couple that argues they have a right to have three children, since they are affluent enough to provide for them, recognizes only their own situation in determining their family size. The woman who maintains that she must bear a third child rather than adopt one is determining her action in terms of what is most gratifying for her emotionally. There is a tendency to limit thought about the question to "the needs of me and my house."

This drives a wedge between the personal and social dimensions of the population control problem. It also defines too narrowly the scope of information to be included in making decisions about family size.

We have discussed certain basic values regarding nature, procreation, and individualism which contribute to an American perspective on population. This paradigm is inadequate. It exalts procreation as necessary to human fulfillment rather than one dimension through which human fulfillment can be known. It imposes on women a role definition which demands procreation and nurture, and leaves little room for choice. Control of procreation is a dominant theme but it is limited to the needs of the individual's immediate situation, excluding the needs of the larger society. It prevents us from moving to a new conceptualization of the meaning and significance of procreation for ourselves and our world.

What should a new paradigm include? We have spoken of a shift in paradigms. The question is "a shift to what?"

A new paradigm should understand procreation as an event which can be one basic avenue to human fulfillment. It should not be seen, however, as a *necessary* means of fulfillment. The childless couple should be free of societal pressures which sympathizes with or judges them as unfortunate or wrong.

Women should have the opportunity to choose the form of fulfillment that is most appropriate and desirable for themselves. They should be freed from the assumption that the biological experience of bearing children is crucial to a complete and whole life. This is not to deny that procreation can become a central experience in a woman's life. Rather, it suggests that women can be full and creative human beings without bearing children. This is a more radical shift than it may seem at first notice, for it requires that we justify procreation. It gives us the responsibility for rationally cross-examining ourselves to find out why we should bring another child into the world rather than remaining childless or nurturing a child already born.

A new paradigm should be as *inclusive* as possible in considering family size. This means that our consideration should not be limited to individual needs and desires, but should include the needs of society, of the world, of the planet with its social and ecological systems, present and future. Personally, this means that we must move beyond our individualism to a position in which we see ourselves as interdependently related to the larger community, rather than independent of it.

Nowhere is this sense of interdependence more necessary than in our relationship to the ecological sphere. This involves a shift in our view of nature. Nature is now considered an object to be controlled in the interest of our needs. This can be described as a relationship in which man is *over* nature. In the new paradigm man should be seen *within* nature. We are a *part of* rather than *lords and masters over* the natural sphere. This does not deny the need to control nature, but it does demand that control be in accord with the limits as well as the possibilities of the environment.[8]

Finally in a new paradigm, the individual right to bear children need not be denied, but indiscriminate childbearing should be subject to the claims of both the child, and the larger community. Both have rights; the child to a future and the community to regulate itself.

These steps toward a new paradigm might help us to develop both a better understanding and a more inclusive view of procreation and its control. By rethinking our values, we may better enable ourselves to fulfill our responsibilities to our world and its destiny.

VALUES AND CRISIS: THE NATION

5

One of our themes has been that the United States is a part of the global crisis, and that it should grapple with the population problem as one member of a world community. International interdependence makes the world crisis our crisis; its solution is in our interest as a nation. But the transition from national to international concern, from standing above the crisis to seeing oneself as a part of the crisis, is not easy. Here we briefly consider three cultural orientations that form the paradigm that hinders acceptance of this new stance as a nation.

The first concerns technology, the second growth, and the third our image as a chosen people. In each of these we are dealing with American cultural myths that inform our perspective and response as a nation.

73

TECHNOLOGY

Our nation has great faith in technology with the emphasis on the category faith. Technology is intrinsically neither good nor evil. Its moral value lies in its use. Further, there is little question that technology is crucial in dealing with the population problem both for yielding new resources for an increasing population and new techniques for birth control. Americans, however, have moved from the stage in which technology is seen as simply a key variable in dealing with the issue. Our faith says that it will solve the problem and this is where we get into trouble. Technology is no longer seen as a crucial weapon in the struggle but as a *deus ex machina* that will come to our rescue. Thus one person can blithely say that the population question is of grave importance but insist that technology will open the ocean to an untold harvest of food, minerals, and space to meet the demands. And another person can in complete confidence promise that soon the perfect contraceptive (that presumably will eliminate all medical, psychological, social, and cultural problems associated with our present means of contraception) will be ready for distribution. When this type of assurance is dominant, we are in trouble. For the seriousness of the situation has been glossed over with unquestioned faith in technology. That faith blinds us to the reality of a breaking bough and a crashing cradle.[1]

Further, it clouds the fact that technology itself contributes to the crisis. As we have observed, the individual in a technological society draws more heavily on the world and its resources than his brother in a less developed country. Yet an unreflecting faith covers our guilt. It hides the negative effects of technology on population.

GROWTH

The second myth is growth. It is fed by a doctrine of progress and a general sense that increase, development, enlargement, and bigness are intrinsically good. At the national level, an increasing GNP is viewed automatically as a sign of progress. Increase, wherever or however it happens, is considered good. No one questions the increasing range of gadgetry. It is a concrete symbol of our genius. The electric can opener and the electric knife are simply minor milestones in an endless cobbled street of inventions. The transportation industry lauds plans for the SST though its cost in air and noise pollution calls it sharply into question. On a three mile stretch of a Minneapolis thoroughfare five neoned hamburger houses and two pizza parlors are erected in a five year span and civic pride is in order. A small Missouri city levels acres of huge oak trees to accommodate a shopping center. The Pentagon reaches for weaponry figured to overkill to the nth power and it is all considered good—it is growth.

The power of the myth feeds the nation's understanding of population. We have already noted that certain analysts see population growth as a necessary condition for the society's continued prosperity. It is symbolized in a machine used at the state fair which ticks off the number of new Americans born each hour for the viewer's delight and pleasure. It shows up in the feeling of pleasure Americans have in living in one of the "top ten cities" in the nation. It can be seen in reports from the Department of Commerce which have periodically applauded population growth.

In sum, population growth is a national corollary to the syndrome of growth to which Americans are so tenaciously committed. This poses an interesting paradox with regard to family size. For even though individual families may for a variety of reasons choose to have a small family, the image of America as a growing population which can continue to grow indefinitely is a well-rooted ideal. There may be personal reasons for keeping our family size small, but this is not linked to the overall accent of the society. It is not difficult to see the danger in this situation. For if a couple finds that their economic and social situation will support having three or four children, the growth ideal rooted in society's values simply provides further justification. The growth myth makes it difficult to see the problem of family size as a serious national issue.

It also inhibits our coming to terms with the global crisis. Our growth-colored glasses filter out the fact that there is not enough to sustain unlimited human life. We assume that growth is a given. To move outside of that myth and see scarcity in the world is not easy.

The problem is that this myth continually reassures us that growth is good and inevitable. Growth as such is neither good nor bad. The goodness or badness of growth is determined by what is increasing and the effects of the increase. To overlook the possible dangers of growth because of the assumption that all growth is good is to flirt with disaster.

THE CHOSEN PEOPLE

A third myth is America's self-image as the chosen people.[2] Present in the nation from its birth, it is complex and deeply rooted in the American religious character. As an Old Testament motif which found rich soil in English Puritanism, it became a fundamental symbol of an American people who found little difficulty in identifying themselves as the New Israel, as the Chosen Race of God, as the people given by God a special place "among the nations."

This myth has cut both ways: it has given the nation a sense of mission and purpose, but it has also fathered the demonic by justifying national and racial imperialism. The late 19th century shows how well the ideology bore its imprint of this attitude. Few historians or theologians of that time did not see the "Anglo-American race" as the people God had chosen to carry to the nations the meaning of American democracy and Christianity.[3] Manifest destiny was nursed at the breast of this myth.

In framing our relationship to other nations this myth provided an ideological prism through which America sees itself as the nation to save the nations, as the messenger carrying salvific balm. Thus Andrew Jackson saved New Orleans, Teddy Roosevelt saved Cuba, the Sergeant Yorks saved Europe and the world for democracy, and now we pace the "free world" as guardian and truant officer. The myth feeds our sense of superiority, setting us apart from the inferior nations of the world. It bears, sustains, and perpetuates a dichotomy in which we see ourselves as strong and righteous, the others as weak and wrong.

The dilemma this poses is obvious. We are a powerful nation with an operative form of democracy and at least some good will for other nations who stand in need. We are thus destined to act out roles consonant with our condition. According to the myth, however, we are not actually involved in the play; America is the hero that enters in the last act to resolve the situation. We are not really a part of the drama, interacting with other nations in an unfolding plot. We stand offstage observing, choosing when and where we shall enter and exit. The analogy with the population problem should be evident.

We stand above the population crisis. The crisis, Americans maintain, is in Asia and Latin America. It belongs to the irresponsible who once again must be saved from their own ineptness and policy shortsightedness. We could paraphrase, "who has not felt in his breast, how long O India, how long, must we tolerate your blindness." The population crisis is out there, not here. It is their crisis, not ours.

The myth hinders a view of our part in the problem. It hides our responsibility to share our technical and economic resources with others in an attempt to solve the problem.

But the myth of the chosen people has made another negative contribution. In making us the superior people, it has cloaked us in an aura of sacredness. A sacred people by definition constitutes the caste of the benevolent and the generous, the fair and the just. In such a role we are blinded to our own true selves. We are the regenerates, not the reprobates. The famine, starvation, and disease out there are not ours and not of our making. We do not see that we consume the protein, the minerals, the food staples at the expense of other people. We do not see that we are the major source of a pollution that threatens the ecological balance. We do not see that we, as the citizens of a technological and affluent society, use and waste many times more than any of our brothers in the rest of the world, except for isolated pockets of the privileged.

To the contrary, we tend to see the American child as a gift to the world. To see it otherwise would be to see all children as equally deserving. We see our nation as a gift to the world. To see it otherwise would be to see it as one among the many, both demonic and good and always interdependent.

The myths and beliefs we have dealt with are not the only factors that contribute to the view of reality we have described. But they do help frame the paradigm through which that reality is created and sustained. They are forces which must be confronted.

In a new paradigm for the nation's response to the world, we need to recognize the crisis in our own society —how it affects us and how we affect other societies. We are a part of the crisis, both in its cause and its effects.

Regarding technology, the new paradigm must subordinate once again man's tools to man and release him from bondage to his servant. This requires a basic reaffirmation of belief in a man who serves the welfare of man rather than the welfare of his products. To the Christian, it means that we respond to the neighbor's needs rather than worshipping our own finite processes and creations.

A new paradigm must move us to the point where we see ourselves as part of the world community—not as the star but as one contributor among many. We should take a stance of international self-interest in which we see ourselves as part of the crisis, bearing responsibility for constructive action. It is this to which we are called as a nation.

THE NECESSITY FOR ACTION

6

In this study we have argued that the population crisis confronting the world threatens the possibility of our own annihilation. In response to this reality, individuals and nations have seen through glasses darkly. The crisis is out there somewhere, a distance away, unclear on a horizon of crises. And in the distance it seems resolvable. Time, technology, God—one of them will answer and we will be saved. Yet time runs out; technology, the primitive tool of a still primitive species, tills fields on other landscapes; and God, who made man free, gave no promise that he would save us from choosing self-destruction.

Thus an epilog of doomsday is tempting, but doomsday prediction is too easy and incomplete. We have also maintained that we do have the power to clarify, analyze, and act in a responsible fashion. We can recognize, understand, and respond. The crisis can be answered.

The problem is that the crisis we have attempted to define has *not* been answered. No encompassing social policy exists at either a national or international level. Programs are minimal, and genuine debate over social policy, though present within the society among concerned groups, does not really exist where it is most necessary—in the legislative halls of Congress.

In the face of this situation, we have explored cultural beliefs and values as one roadblock to an adequate response. We have concluded that new paradigms of beliefs are necessary. New paradigms alone will not bring about the necessary individual, social, economic, and political responses that are necessary, but they can provide the informing vision and values that must be present before those necessary responses will occur. They are essential to framing a moral response to the problem.

Let us turn to the question of moral decision-making and isolate, in light of our discussion of the crises and the new paradigms, certain moral guidelines we should consider in determining family size.

1. We should begin with the assumption that we do not stand beyond the crises but are a part of it as individuals and as a nation. Because of that, we have the moral responsibility to justify the number of children we choose to have. We live in a world of overpopulation, rather than population scarcity.

2. Contraceptives as a rational means of family planning are a necessity. Responsible control does not occur unless such means are used.

3. In making the choice regarding family size, we should recognize that human fulfillment is not dependent on childbearing or childrearing. Rather it is one among many ways to fulfillment.

4. In determining family size, we should consider more than our own immediate individual situation. The claims of the broader community and the environmental spheres are equally imperative and must be considered carefully.

These guidelines are not exclusive. Others could be delineated. But these do frame fundamental guidelines for moral deliberation.

Are there theological grounds for this response? I believe that there are, and they are deeply rooted in a Christian view of man. Let us sketch certain of its major motifs.

In the second creation story of Genesis, the human species comes last in the creative process—out of the dust, to return to the dust.

To translate this perspective, we can suggest that man is part of a creation he did not begin and does not ultimately control. For man is not God; man is a creature, the finite one within the processes of a dynamic universe. Man is a part of creation rather than its lord and master —a part of a greater whole interacting with parts not of his making. Man is interdependent and interrelated, not autonomous and independent.

Man is unique in this creation. He has been given the power to transcend the interaction and observe the process unfolding. He sees himself and what he does. He reflects on it and can act in the face of its demands. He is given freedom, and in that freedom power to reason and to choose. This transcendence, however, is not a freedom to separate himself from creation as its exploiter, but to consciously relate to it in a morally responsible fashion. He has been separated from the brother, the tribe, the environment, but for the purpose of morally responding to them. The locus of the Christian moral life rests in relationships to the total creation, and the fulfillment of that life comes out of these relationships. It is the interaction he has with the other that is crucial. There he knows that which saves and that which destroys; there he experiences wholeness and brokenness, grace and judgment, the divine and the demonic.

This relational character of the faith is deeply embedded in its history. The Old Testament is the story of a relationship between a people and God. The quality and integrity of that relationship was of ultimate significance. In the New Testament this theme is reiterated in the moral imperative that man should love God and his neighbor.

In this context, the determination of morality or immorality, rightness or wrongness depends on the intent and effect of the individual's actions on the other. As he enters into relationship with his brother, his community, his environment, he must weigh his intentions and their implications for those parties. He must accept responsibility for his action and its effect on them. In making a decision on procreation, therefore, his reasoning must focus on the meaning and significance that procreation will have for the realms to which he is intricately and interdependently related. Moral responsibility begins with a question: what effect will my action have on the other subjects to which I am related?

If this has been a motif in Christianity, it has also been the victim of circumscription at the hands of the faithful. We have acted in light of our self-interest to define our boundaries narrowly. We have been willing to say that our actions should be weighed, but only in terms of their effect on certain chosen parties. Thus family size has been the subject of careful deliberation in terms of how it might affect a selected few—the individuals directly concerned—but not other persons, groups, or realms of creation. Or we have predetermined the rightness or wrongness of action and circumvented the process of interaction as an influence on our decisions. Using this approach, we have said that procreation is good and therefore should be accommodated regardless of conditions in the society or the world.

What must replace this response is a recognition of man's place as a part of creation in which his actions are to be judged in terms of their consequences for the created order of man and nature. This gives man the responsibility to understand that order and the significance of his actions.

There is an awesomeness in this responsibility. It means that the weighing of appropriate action is a necessity, not an option. This weighing does not lead to conclusions applicable for all epochs, only to conclusions applicable to our own historical era. In the Old Testament a writer issues a call: "Be fruitful and multiply." That mandate was appropriate to an era when man was pitted against the possibility of extinction. In our present world, however, the situation is reversed. In the face of an ecological crisis, of resource depletion, and a world of inadequate social and economic institutions all strained by overpopulation, extinction may well be the consequence of our multiplication. We may breed ourselves to death. Given this situation, moral responsibility calls for population control undertaken in light of the total social and natural environment and its needs.

These are the concerns to consider for determination of family size.

NOTES

CHAPTER 1

1. Paul Ehrlich, *The Population Bomb* (New York: Ballantine Books, 1968).

2. Report of the Board of Social Ministry, Bulletin of Reports, Fifth Biennial Convention of the Lutheran Church in America. Minneapolis, 1970, p. 297.

3. David Lyle, "The Human Race Has, Maybe, Thirty-five Years Left," *Esquire Magazine,* Planned Parenthood/World Population reprint, 515 Madison Ave., New York, New York.

4. Ben Wattenberg, "The Nonsense Explosion," *New Republic,* April 4 and 11, 1970.

5. Jan Lenica and Alfred Sauvy, *Population Explosion, Abundance or Famine* (New York: Dell Publishing Co., Inc., 1962), p. 22. This book provides a general historical sketch of major events in population history.

6. Henry Wallich, "Population Growth," *Newsweek,* June 29, 1970, p. 70.

7. Niel J. Smelser and James A. Davis, editors, *Sociology* (Englewood Cliffs, N.J.; Prentice-Hall, Inc. © 1969), pp. 47-48. By permission of Prentice-Hall, Inc.

8. Dear Abby, "Don't Put on Heirs," *Minneapolis Star*, July 17, 1970, p. 63. Reprinted from the *Dear Abby* column by Abigail Van Buren, © 1970, Chicago Tribune-New York News Syndicate, Inc.

9. Ralph Potter, *War and Moral Discourse* (Richmond, Virginia: John Knox Press, 1969), pp. 23-24.

10. David M. Heer, *Society and Population* (Englewood Cliffs, N. J.: Prentice-Hall, Inc., 1968). This book reviews the three following theoretical frameworks as well as other important categories and hypotheses significant to population analysis.

11. Lenica and Sauvy, p. 26.

12. Smelser and Davis, p. 50. For a more comprehensive treatment of the theory of Demographic Transition see Karl Sax, *The World's Exploding Population* (Boston: Beacon Press, 1955), chapter 3, and for a discussion and critique of the theory's limitations see David Heer, *op. cit.*, chapter 1.

13. Reproduced from *Fortune Magazine* in *Population Chronicle*, no. 2, September 1969, p. 5.

14. Sylvia Porter, *Minneapolis Tribune*, July 1, 1970, p. 7. Copyright 1970 Field Enterprises, Inc. Courtesy of Publishers-Hall Syndicate.

15. For a brief, concise summary of one type of sociological study on population see Smelser and Davis, "A Field Experiment on Family Planning," *Sociology*, pp. 8-10. Also see David Heer, *op. cit.*, who provides a more complete analysis from the sociological perspective.

16. See William Petersen's, *The Politics of Population* (Garden City; New York: Doubleday and Co., Inc., 1964), for a study of the relationship of political factors and population. See also *Congressman's Report*, Morris K. Udall, July 30, 1969, vol. VIII, no. 7.

17. See Paul and Anne Ehrlich, *Population, Resources, Environment* (San Francisco: W. H. Freeman, 1970), for a recent examination of the ecological and technological relationships to population.

18. The classical study tracing the history of contraceptive techniques is that of Norman Himes, *Medical History of Contraception* (Baltimore: The Williams and Wilkens Co., 1938).

19. See William Goode, *World Revolution and Family Patterns* (Glencoe, Ill.: Free Press, 1963) for a discussion of this specific problem, pp. 52-53.

20. See Gibson Winter, *Elements for a Social Ethic* (New York: Macmillan Co., 1966)

21. See Wilson Yates, "American Protestantism and Birth Control: An Examination of Shifts within a Major Religious Value Orientation," (Ph.D. diss., Harvard University, April 1968). In this thesis the value orientation of Protestantism regarding birth control is traced in American history.

22. Arthur Dyck, "Religious Factors in the Population Problem," *Religious Situation,* 1968 (Boston: Beacon Press, 1968), chapter 4, pp. 177-178.

23. Two major studies which provide presentations of Protestants and Roman Catholic stances on the question of population control are Richard M. Fagley, *The Population Explosion and Christian Responsibility* (New York: Oxford, 1960), and John Noonan, *Contraception* (Cambridge: Harvard Press, 1965). A further statement which deals more specifically with the Protestant's problem in responding to the issue is "Protestant Parochialism and the Population Problem," by Ralph Potter in *Special Background Papers for the Alma College American Assembly on the Population Dilemma,* April 6-9, 1967. See also Alan Graebner, "Birth Control and the Lutherans, The Missouri Synod as a Case Study," in *Journal of Social History,* vol. 2, no. 4, Summer 1969.

CHAPTER 2

1. Robert Heilbroner, "Ecological Armageddon," *New York Review of Books,* April 23, 1970, p. 4.

2. James Ridgeway, "Depopulants," *Hardtimes,* June 23 and 30, 1969, articulates the Third World attitude. The new president of Mexico, Luis Escheverria Alvarez, who is no revolutionary, presents a position long held in Latin American politics that "to govern is to populate" when he referred to Mexico as "a country whose demographic expansion we neither want to nor can arrest. On the contrary we should encourage it . . ." (At the present rate Mexico's population of 14 million will double in 20 years), quoted by N. A. Haverstock and Richard C. Schroeder, "Against Babies? Not Mexico's New President," *Minneapolis Tribune,* September 18, 1970.

3. See Reinhold Niebuhr, *Man's Nature and His Communities* (New York: Charles Scribner's Sons, 1965), chapter 1. Here he defines his own realist posture as well as critiqueing Morgenthau's.

4. *Population Chronicle,* "Summary Report," no. 1, August 1969, p. 5.

5. Reinhold Niebuhr, in *Reinhold Niebuhr on Politics*. Edited by Harry R. Davis and Robert C. Good. (New York: Charles Scribner's Sons, 1960), p. 336

6. *Ibid.*

7. Robert McNamara, quoted in *Population Chronicle*, no. 2, September 1969, p. 6, from a speech delivered at Notre Dame.

8. Quoted by Robert Heilbroner, p. 3.

9. Wayne H. Davis, "Thoughts on Feeding the Hungry, More or Less People," *New Republic*, June 20, 1970, p. 19. Used by permission.

10. Lester Brown, quoted in *Population Chronicle*, no. 1, August 1969, pp. 1-2.

11. See Lord Ritchie Calder, "Polluting the Environment," *Center Magazine*, May 1969, p. 11.

12. B. R. Sen, *Food, Population and Development* (Rome: Food and Agriculture Organization of the United Nations, 1965), pp. 7-8.

13. p. 24

14. p. 9.

15. Paul Ehrlich, *The Population Bomb* (New York: Ballantine Books, 1968), p. 133. Used by permission.

CHAPTER 3

1. Ben Wattenberg, "The Nonsense Explosion," *New Republic*, April 4 & 11, 1970, p. 19. The figures are taken from Wattenberg's essay with the exception of the 1936 figure of 75.8 which is more precise than his rounded figure of 76. The revised figure is given in the quote of note 2. Furthermore, Wattenberg does not acknowledge the upward shift now emerging.

2. A Report prepared for the American Friends Service Committee, *Who Shall Live?* (New York: Hill and Wang, 1969), p. 88. Used by permission.

3. *Population Chronicle*, "Population News and Notes," no. 3, March 1970, p. 4.

4. Wattenberg, p. 20

5. Herman Miller quoted in "Dangers Seen in Zero Population Growth," by H. Erich Heineman, *Minneapolis Tribune*, June 7, 1970, p. 12A.

6. Wattenberg, p. 22

7. Hendrick Houthakker quoted in "Dangers Seen in Zero Population Growth," p. 12A.

8. Robert Heilbroner, "Ecological Armageddon," *New York Review of Books,* April 23, 1970, p. 6. See also Kenneth E. Boulding, "The Economics of the Coming Spaceship Earth," in *Environmental Handbook.* Edited by Garrett De Bell. (New York: Ballantine Books, 1970), pp. 96-101

9. Wattenberg, p. 21

10. Wayne H. Davis, "Thoughts on Feeding the Hungry, More or Less People," *New Republic,* June 20, 1970, p. 20.

11. Emilio Q. Daddario quoted by David Lyle in "The Human Race Has, Maybe, Thirty-five Years Left," *Esquire Magazine,* Planned Parenthood/World Population Reprint, 515 Madison Ave., New York, N.Y

12. The following quote extends the argument regarding space and pinpoints its complexity. "The population of the United States, by the year 2000, is expected to grow by another one hundred million people, most of whom will be crowded into urban centers that already hold 70% of the population on less than 10% of the nation's land." From *Who Shall Live?* p. 7. Used by permission.

13. Judith Blake, "Population Policy for Americans: Is the Government Being Misled?" *Science,* May 2, 1969, p. 524. In a report to the Advisory Council of Planned Parenthood /World Population reported in *Population Chronicle,* no. 3, March 1970, p. 4, Charles Westhoff argues that data shows that the poor have more children but desire less: "15% of births to non-poor parents were wanted, the figure is 23% for the near-poor and 37% for the poor." This provides some balance to the Blake argument and does suggest that family planning programs of a voluntary nature are still in order in dealing with all groups as opposed to stringent legislation.

14. David Heer, *Society and Population* (Englewood Cliffs, N.J.: Prentice-Hall, Inc., 1968), p. 99.

15. See Jean Mayer, "Affluence: the Fifth Horseman of the Apocalypse, A Conversation with Jean Mayer and T. George Harris," *Psychology Today,* January 1970, p. 50. Mayer states: "It's the rich . . . who wreak the environment. Rich people occupy much more space, consume more of each natural resource, disturb the ecology more, litter the landscape with bottles and paper and pollute more land, air, and water with chemical, thermal, and radioactive waste."

16. Quoted in *Contact,* the Newsletter of Congressman, Joseph E. Karth, Summer 1970, p. 4.

17. Paul Ehrlich, *The Population Bomb* (New York: Ballantine Books, 1968), p. 133.

CHAPTER 4

1. This view of paradigm change draws on Thomas Kuhn's analysis of paradigms. See Thomas Kuhn, *The Structure of Scientific Revolutions* (Chicago: University of Chicago Press, 1962).

2. This definition of culture and its use in this essay is drawn from Talcott Parsons, *Societies, Evolutionary and Comparative Perspectives* (Englewood Cliffs, N.J.: Prentice-Hall, Inc., 1966), pp. 9 ff.

3. Max Weber, *The Protestant Ethic and the Rise of Capitalism* (New York: Charles Scribner's Sons, 1958). In the following discussion I have followed closely the interpretation given to Weber's view by Talcott Parsons in his study, *The Structure of Social Action* (Glencoe, Ill.: Free Press, 1949), pp. 516 ff.

4. See Wilson Yates, "American Protestantism and Birth Control: An Examination of Shifts within and Major Religious Value Orientation," (Ph.D. diss., Harvard University, April 1968).

5. Mary Truact, "Status of Women Faculty on the Twin Cities Campus," Minnesota Planning and Counseling Center for Women, University of Minnesota.

6. For a basic work which gives detailed attention to individualism in the context of America's development, see Ralph Henry Gabriel, *The Course of American Democratic Thought* (New York: The Ronald Press, 1956). See also *Innocence and Power, Individualism in Twentieth Century America*. Edited by Gordon Mills. (Austin, Tex.: University of Texas Press, 1965).

7. See Robert Bellah, "American Civil Religion," *Daedelus*, Winter 1967.

8. See Ian McHarg, *Design with Nature* (Garden City, N.Y.: The Natural History Press, 1969), He develops the notion of how we can design with nature in such a fashion that our control of it is in accord with nature's own possibilities and limitations. His position is insightful for what we are suggesting in this discussion.

CHAPTER 5

1. See Lynn White Jr., "The Historical Roots of Our Ecological Crisis," *Environmental Handbook* (New York: Ballantine Books, 1970), pp. 12-26, for a discussion of the cultural legitimation of technology and the need for a new cultural orientation towards it.

2. Winthrop Hudson, *American Protestantism* (Chicago: University of Chicago Press, 1961), p. 62 ff. Hudson picks up this theme of the chosen people in American Protestantism and America in general.

3. See Thomas F. Gossett, *Race: The History of an Idea in America* (New York: Schocken Books, 1965). This study lifts up the chosen people motif and its implications for race in America. See also David Noble, *Historians Against History* (Minneapolis: University of Minnesota Press, 1965). Noble explores the theme in the writers of American history showing how the myth permeates historical writing itself.

FOR FURTHER READING

The following books and articles are recommended for further reading. Some have been used in this discussion, while others explore areas we did not consider.

Peter Fryer, *The Birth Controllers* (New York: Stein and Day, 1965). This book gives a popular historical introduction to the emergence of the birth control movement in America. It is written in a lively style drawing on many of the colorful events surrounding the efforts of birth control reform.

Jan Lenica and Alfred Sauvy, *Population Explosion, Abundance or Famine* (New York: Dell Publishing Co., Inc., 1962). This short book complemented by captivating visual presentations of drawings provides a brief historical overview of population development throughout history and certain of the salient factors that have brought us to our present crisis.

Roger Revelle, editor, "Historical Population Studies," *Daedelus*, Spring 1968. In this volume of the *Journal of The American Academy of Arts and Sciences*, essays by leading population analysts explore historical factors which help interpret the history of population growth and its interaction with other sectors of society. This is one of the best collections of such essays and provides a wealth of information on the meaning of population to a society's own development and health.

David M. Heer, *Society and Population* (Englewood Cliffs, N.J.: Prentice-Hall, Inc., 1968). This study gives an excellent introduction to the study of population. It gives the reader basic theories and concepts important to population analysis as well as a summary of major studies in the field.

Population Chronicle is a publication of The Population Council and the International Institute for the Study of Human Reproduction, Columbia University. Copies of this monthly publication can be obtained by writing to Population Chronicle c/o The Population Council, 245 Park Avenue, New York City, New York 10017. This publication reviews current developments in population studies and programs. It is a readable and helpful journal which states that ". . . it is intended to give its readers sound information in a non-technical manner."

Paul Ehrlich, *The Population Bomb* (New York, Ballantine Books, 1968). Written in a non-technical, lively, and polemical style, it provides concrete suggestions for the individual in responding to the population crisis as well as an analysis of the crisis. For a more detailed analysis see Paul and Anne Ehrlich, *Population, Resources, Environment* (San Francisco: W. H. Freeman, 1970).

94

S. J. Behrman, Leslie Corsa, Jr. and Ronald Freedman, editors, *Fertility and Family Planning* (Ann Arbor, Michigan: University of Michigan Press, 1970). This study provides articles on a significant dimension of population studies and is important for an overview of the world issues as well as approaches being used in responding to the population problem. It contains 19 papers delivered at the University of Michigan in 1967 at a population conference.

Materials dealing specifically with the religious factor both in terms of beliefs and institutions include the following: Richard M. Fagley, *The Population Explosion and Christian Responsibility* (New York: Oxford, 1960), which explores particularly the Protestant position in contrast to other communions; John Noonan, *Contraception* (Harvard: Cambridge, Massachusetts: Belknap Press, 1965). which traces the shifting Roman Catholic positions on birth control; two essays from *Daedelus*, Summer 1959, "Protestant Ethics and Population Control" by John C. Bennett and "The Catholic Position on Population Control" by John L. Thomas, S.J. In *The Lutheran*, June 3, 1970, an article by Marjorie Bracher, "The Two-Child Family, Facing the Population Crisis," summarizes the argument for the two-child family and what a number of churches' responses have been to the population problem. In a volume to be published in 1971, *Freedom, Coercion and the Life Sciences*, edited by Daniel Callahan, et al., articles by two Christian ethicists, Ralph Potter and Arthur Dyck will be of special interest relative to ethical concerns regarding population policy. An essay dealing with the response of one Protestant group to birth control provides a good case study of a denomination's position and behavior: Alan Graebner, "Birth Control and the Lutherans, The Missouri Synod as a Case Study," *Journal of Social History*, vol. 2, no. 4, Summer 1969. A report prepared for the American Friends Service Committee, *Who Shall Live?* discusses the question of birth control and abortion. The report is in book form (New York: Hill and Wang, 1970). It is a very helpful study in isolating many of the crucial ethical issues. See Arthur Dyck, "Religious Factors in the Population Problem," *The Religious Situation, 1968* (Boston: Beacon Press, 1968), for a good resumé of studies on the relationship of religion to population and a constructive case for understanding the role of religion.

www.ingramcontent.com/pod-product-compliance
Lightning Source LLC
Chambersburg PA
CBHW050216270326
41914CB00003BA/431